John Patrick

A Century of select Psalms, and portions of the Psalms of David

Especially those of praise turned into metre and fitted to the usuall tunes in parish

churches

John Patrick

A Century of select Psalms, and portions of the Psalms of David
Especially those of praise turned into metre and fitted to the usuall tunes in parish churches

ISBN/EAN: 9783741103179

Manufactured in Europe, USA, Canada, Australia, Japa

Cover: Foto ©Lupo / pixelio.de

Manufactured and distributed by brebook publishing software (www.brebook.com)

John Patrick

A Century of select Psalms, and portions of the Psalms of David

With Harp and
Heart I sing.

A
CENTURY
Of Select
PSALMS,

And Portions of the

PSALMS of DAVID,

Especially those of Praise

Turned into Metre and fitted to the
usuall Tunes in Parish Churches.

By *JOHN PATRICK,*
D. D.

HAMBURG,
Printed by Thomas Wiering, Ao. 1692.

PREFACE
TO THE
READER.

WERE it not that the Singing-Psalms, commonly used in Churches, labour under the Prejudice of an ill Translation, whose dress is course and homely, the Metre rugged and unequal, being patched up with little care, the words many of them out of use and scarce intelligible, without fancy and sometimes, which is worse, without any sense; I cannot think that any sober, devout person, would decry or sleight the singing of them in the Church: Wherein

)o(though

though the common People cannot attain, in this, more than in other matters, to much skill or art; yet however they seem to me to be employed more affectionately in this, than in any other part of the Service: and considering that praising God is the most excellent part of it, by the same reason that the Apostle prefers Charity before Faith and Hope, because when they cease to be of use, this remains for ever, even in Heaven it self; it may seem very reasonable to afford the people all furtherance and assistence to the better performance of that, to which they have already a laudable propension.

I confess there are discouragements to undertake such a work, and

and particularly that, which some others have deservedly complained of, viz. the ungracefulness of the Measures of our Common Tunes: which I think happens to have been the worst chosen of any Metre extant in any language, and scarce admits, when words are fitted to them, of any Elegancy; which therefore the Excellent Poets of our own have balked, and chosen in their Translations, to use Pindaries or other measures of their own fancying, wherein, without being so much straitned, they had more scope for their flights and Elegancies. But since the people cannot be wound up to them, he that intends their benefit, must condescend, and take, as he finds it, the Metre they are accuſtomed to ; and fit ſuch words to them as they can under-ſtand, and may convey naturally and eaſily into their minds that pious ſenſe which every where breaths in the Pſalms of David And perhaps this may be a harder task to doe well, than he that has not try'd it would imagine : eſpe-cially when he muſt not take lea-ve to Paraphraſe largely in ſtrains of his own, but muſt keep cloſely, tho' not to every word, yet to the ſenſe of the Text as it lies before him.

This has been attempted , I know, by many, but, I think, not ſo ſucceſsfully as might have been wiſht. For the moſt have plain-ly miſcarried, by tying themſelves too ſtrictly , I had almoſt ſaid ſuperftitioufly, to the words of the English Text, which in a Thousand places cannot be made to fall Naturally, without botching, into verfe; fo that there is little more of Poetry in them, than mere Rhime.

When I obferved thefe things, tho' at firft onely intended to make a Collection of Pfalms out of others, for the ufe of that Society to which I relate (where we are bound by the Orders of the Houfe, upon Sundays and Feftivals and the Eves of them, to fing the Pfalms to an Organ, tho' without a Quire) I altered my thoughts, and refolved to try, as others had done before me, fo to fit the Pfalms to the common Tunes, that the vulgar might bear their part in them, and the more intelligent and skilfull migth

might not have reason to despise
this part of the Service. Which
design whether I have performed,
I must leave others to judge; o-
nely desiring when they do so, to
remember that this was my end,
and not to sed up for a Poet.

And now to give the Reader
some account of my manner of
proceeding herein; Because (for
the reason before given) I resolved not to tie up my self strictly
to the use of the words of the English Text, unless they would
fall in naturally, but rather to clear the phrases by a short Paraphra-
se, tho' still keeping to the sense;
I therefore consulted the Criticks
and other Expositors upon places
of difficulty, and especially the
Pharaphrases of the Learned Doc-
tor

ror Hammond and Amyraldus. I
have endeavoured to suit my Version to the strain of the Psalms,
which are very different; some
more humble and plain, best sui-
ted to David's afflictive Com-
plaints, or to those Psalms that instruct mens manners: Others are
more lofty, elegant and poetical;
as when he sets out the works of
God, his Creation and Providence, or the perfections of the Almighty Ruler of the World; or
prophetically describes things that
relate to the Messiah. Instances
of which may be seen in Psalm
23. 29. 45. 65. 91. 93. 96. 104.
139. not to mention many others.

I foresee two Objections against
my method of proceeding; which
I shall briefly endeavour to satisfie.
The

The one is, that I have left so many
Psalms untranslated : the other,
that I have taken at other times o-
nely some portions of Psalms, and
left out many Verses in those I have
translated. In Answer to both
which, I think it may suffice to return; That in the choice I have
made, I considered and pitched u-
pon those Psalms or portions of
them which were most proper and
of most general use to us Christians.
Such are Psalms of Thanksgiving,
or of Petition for mercies we all
need, or that instruct us in our Duty. But I balked those whose aspect
was upon David's personal troubles, or Israel's particular condition. or related to the Jewish and le-
gal Oeconomy, or are prophetical
of the Nations they should subdue,
or respected their deliverances, or
such

such as refer not to us, but by a more difficult Accommodation; or where they express a temper not so sutable to the mild and gentle spirit of the Gospel, such as our Saviour repressed in his Disciples, not allowing imprecations of vengeance against our Enemies, but rather praying for them; especially when that prophetick spirit do's not now rest upon us, that did upon David. so also such Psalms as are of very Artificial contrivance in the Hebrew, the Verses beginning with the several Letters of the Alphabet, and the phrases with great Art varied, tho' containing the same repeated sense, which cannot be imitated so well in other Tongues, many Verses in them are left out; as among others in the 37th Psalm, and especially in the 119th Psalm which the-

re-

refore I have contracted into six
parts: I might also add, that I have
sometimes omitted a few Verses
that preface to a Psalm. If these rea-
sons will be allowed me, then I sup-
pose there will be very little found
either in whole Psalms or pieces of
them, that is not translated. If this
satisfie not, I have onely one thing
farther to offer, which methinks
may. That I desire onely that I may
have the same favour that is granted to every Parish Clark; who in
setting the Psalms, is not wont to
run through them in order, nor to
appoint at all times a whole one to
be sung, but onely such portions of
them as are suitable to the occasion, or to the time allotted not for
this alone, but for other services to
be performed in the Congregatiõ:
And if I had said no more, I know
not

not why I may not take liberty to
pick and chuse portions of Pſalms,
as well as he. I have nothing more to add, unleſs it be fit to mention, that I have put very many
of the Pſalms into the Metre of the
Hundred Pſalm, which meaſure, as
well as the Tune, I judge to be the
beſt we have: but for thoſe that
may be of another mind, I have
compleyed ſo far, as to repeat the
far greater number of ſuch Pſalms
in the commoner Metre: and that
I know but of one very hard word,
that may trouble an ordinary Reader, which he will find in the firſt
line of the 127th Pſalm, viz. the
word Architect, which ſignifies a
Maſter -Builder, and I hope he
will not meet with ſuch another
through-out the whole work.

Pſalm

Psalm I.

BLest is the Man, that walks not where
　　Ungodly Councells guide,
Nor stands in sinful ways; Nor sits
　　With those, who God deride
But in the Law of God' the Lord
　　Hath fixt his whole delight
And in that Law doth exercise
　　Himselfe both Day and Night.

He shall be like a Tree, which grows
　　Close by the Rivers side
Whose loaded Boughs in Fruits return
　　Their Tribute to the Tide
No blasting wind, nor biting frost
　　Shall make his Leaves drop down:
What ever work he takes in hand
　　Happy success shall Crown.

But with the wicked 'tis not so;
　　They are as Chaff out cast.
Scatter'd and made the restless sport
　　Of every wanton Blast,
Unlike in Life, unlike shall be
　　The ends which on them wait
Whilst these in Judgment cannot stand
　　And those are prais'd ith' Gate.

God doth the purer wayes approve
　　Which his Redeemed tread
But Paths perverse do surely down
　　To death and horrour lead.

Psalm

Psalm I.

(To the 100 *Psalm Tune.*)

BLest is the Man whose vertuous steps
No wicked Counsels lead aside;
Nor stands in Sinners ways; nor sits
where God and Goodness men deride.

But on the Laws Divine his love
Is plac'd, his Souls entire delight;
On these his mind is fix'd by Day,
On these his wakefull thoughts by Night.

He like a Tree, from living streams
Derives his sap and kindly juice;
His leaves are ever fresh and green,
His branches timely fruits produce.

No cross events shall blast his hopes,
Nor spoil the pleasures of his mind;
Whilst the ungodly are dispers'd
Like chaff, by every stormy wind.

Tho' Sinners here may pass for Saints,
And vile Hyprocrisie for Grace;
Their Guilt, when jug'd, will find no Plea,
Nor they among the just a place.

God will reward the Just mens works,
As he approves the ways they tread;
But the smooth paths of Sinners, down
To death and to damnation lead.

A   Psalm

Pſalm II.

1 WHY do the Heathen Nations rage,
        And fooliſh things ſurmiſe;
2 Kings ſet themſelves againſt their God,
        Rulers his Chriſt deſpiſe?
3 His gentle Government they count
        Their Yoke, his Laws their Chain;
Freedom they'll have without controll,
        No Bands ſhall them reſtrain.

4 But God above will ſcorn their rage,
        Their vain attempts deride;
5 His Pow'r ſhall fright them, and his wrath
        Vex their defeated Pride.
6 For all their ſpite, I've ſet my King
        Securely on his Throne:
7 And, what I had decreed before,
        Proclaim'd him now my Son.

This is the Birth-day of thy Rule,
8   Thy Sceptre I'll advance
O'er all the Earth; the Gentiles give
        For thine inheritance.
9 Thou with an Iron rod ſhal bruiſe
        Their diſobedient Neck;
Like brittle Potſherds, all their powers
        Without reſiſtence break.

10 Let the great Rulers of the World,
        This greater Lord revere;
11 Serve him with cheatfull willingneſs,
        And to diſpleaſe him fear.

12 In low submissions to the Son,
Your happiness does lye;
Then you are safe, when h'es well pleas'd;
When he's provok'd ye dye.

Psalm III.

1 WHat numbers, Lord, against me rise,
And in my troubles boast?
2 That say my hopes in God are vain,
And my Condition lost?
3 But, Lord, I'll glory in thee still,
And on thy Pow'r rely?
Thou shalt defend me as a shield,
And lift my head on high.

4 To thee I cry'd in my distress,
And thou from Heav'n didst hear;
5 Safely I slept without concern,
And wak'd without all fear.
6 Tho' thousands of my Foes conspir'd,
My courage should not fail;
Tho' they besieg'd me, I should be
Secur'd, or else prevail.

7 Arise, and save me, O my God;
For thou hast heretofore
Turn'd back my Enemies with shame,
And broken all their pow'r.
8 Those whom the Lord do's Love and own,
He still will bless and save;
Then let this author of their good,
Their chearfull praises have.

Pfalm IV.

1 HEar me, O Lord, the great fupport
    Of mine Integrity;
Thou haft my former troubles eas'd,
    Now to my Pray'rs draw nigh.

2 Fond men! that would my Glory ftain,
    My Government defpife;
How long will ye purfue vain hopes,
    And pleafe your felves with lies?

3 Know that the Lord do's righteous Men
    With fpecial favour own:
Tho' you defpife me, he ne'er will
    On my Petitions frown.

4 Sin not, but fear; let quiet thoughts
    Inftruct and make you wife;

5 Joyn a pure heart with truft in God
    As the beft Sacrifice.

6 Tho' others in diftruft of thee,
    To other fuccours fly;
Thou art our hope; Lord, caft on us
    A favourable Eye.

7 Thy Love more chears my heart than when
    Their Corn has wifh'd increafe;
Or when a happy Vintage makes
    Their Wine o'erflovv the Prefs.

8 Dovvn vvill I lye in Peace, and fleep
    Shall clofe my vvearied Eyes;
No fears difturb me, vvhilft I knovv
    In God my fafety lies.

Pfalm

Pſalm VI.

(Tho the 100 Pſalm Tune)

1 LOrd, I can ſuffer thy rebukes,
  vvhen thou doſt kindly me chaſtiſe;
But thy fierce vvrath I cannot bear;
O let not that againſt me riſe.

2 Pitty my languiſhing Eſtate;
  And thoſe perplexities I feel,
3 While cruſhed by thy heavy hand,
  O let thy gentler touches heal.

4 Lord, for thy goodneſs ſake, return
  And ſave my life; for in the Grave
5 None can remember thee, nor thou
  Thankſull acknovvlegdments canſt have.

6 See hovv I paſs my vveary dayes
  In ſighs and groanes; and vvhen 'tis night,
  I drovvn my Bed and ſelf in tears:
7 My grief conſumes and dims my ſight.

8 Depart ye vvicked Foes; your hopes
  Are dath'd; for this my mournfull voice,
  Will bring God nearer to mine aid,
  When you come flocking to rejoyce.

9 The Lord hath heard my Pray'r; and thoſe.
10 That gap'd upon me as their prey,
  Will vex themſelves at their defeat,
  And vvith confuſion turn avvay.

Pſalm

Pfalm VI.

(Another metre.)

1 Lord, I can vvel endure, vvhen thou
   Doſt kindly me chaſtiſe ;
 But thy fierce vvrath I cannot bear,
   O let it never riſe.
2 Pity my vveak Eſtate, and thoſe
   Perplexities I feel,
3 While cruſhed by thy hand ; O let
   Thy gentler touches heal.
4 In mercy, Lord, return and ſpare
   My life, for in the grave
5 None can remember thee ; nor thou
   Acknovvledgments can it have.
6 See hovv I paſs my vveary days
   In groans ; and vvhen 'tis night,
 I drovvn my Bed and ſelf in tears ;
7 My grief conſumes my ſight.
8 Depart ye vvicked Foes your hopes
   Are daſh'd, my mournfull voice
 Will bring me help from God, vvhen you
   Come flocking to rejoyce.
9 The Lord hath heard my Pray'r and thoſe
   That gaped for a prey ;
 Vexed at their defeited hopes
   With ſhame ſhall turn avvay.

Pfalm VIII.

1 O Lord our Governour, on Earth
   Thy Name is Excellent ;

Thy

Thy Glory is exalted far
  Above the Firmament.
2 From the vveak Povv'rs of Babes, thou mak'ft
    Thy Victories arife;
  They ftill the Triumphs of thy Foes,
    And fhame thine Enemies.

3 When I to Heav'n, thy glorious vvork,
    Raife mine admiring Eye;
  And there behold the Moon and Stars —
    That beautify the Sky:
4 Lord! vvhat is man, that he fhould have
    In thy kind thoughts a place;
  Why doft thou thus advance and blefs
    His miferable Race?

5 Tho' lovver than the Angels made,
    He vvears a Glorious Crovvn:
6 Thy vvorks belovv all ftoop to him,
    And for their Sov'reign ovvn.
7 The Beafts that in the Paftures feed
    Or in the Defarts lie;
8 Fifhes that move vvithin the Seas,
    And Fovvls beneath the Sky.

9 Thefe are his Slaves; but let not Man
    Difovvn God's Gouvernment;
  Whofe Povv'r do's rule the World vvhofe
      Name,
    Alone is Excellent.

Pfalm

Pſalm IX.

(As the 100 *Pſalm.*)

1 WIth all my Soul I'll bleſs the Lord,
  And all his mighty vvorks proclaim:
2 Gladneſs and Joy ſhall fill my heart,
  Whilſt I ſing praiſes to his Name.

7 Th'Eternal God, from change ſecure,
  Has plac'd his Throne in glorious Light;
8 When he appears to judge the World,
  His ſentence vvill be juſt and right.

9 From him th' oppreſs'd vvill find relief,
  He'll be their refuge in diſtreſs;
10 No good Mans Faith vvas ever ſham'd,
  His Pray'r ne'er vvanted good ſucceſs.

16 God, by the judgments he inflicts,
  Declares his Righteouſneſs to all:
  They that lay trains to hurt the good,
  Set Traps t'occaſion their ovvn fall.

17 Yea Hell the ruine of them vvaits,
  Who God and Juſtice diſregard:
18 When poor mens vvronged Patience
  Obtains ſure reſcue and revvard.

19 Ariſe, O Lord, and interpoſe,
  To blaſt the wickeds good ſucceſs,
20 And by their Terrours make them feel
  They are but Men, and ſo confeſs.

Pſalm

Psalm IX.

(*Another Metre.*)

1 I'Ll bless the Lord with all my Soul,
  And all his works proclaim;
2 Gladness shall fill my heart, whilst I
  Sing praises to his Name.

7 Th' Eternal God has plac'd on high
  His Throne in glorious light:
8 When he appears to judge the World,
  His Sentence will be right.

9 From him th' oppress'd will find reliefe,
  And refuge in distress:
10 No good mens hopes return asham'd,
  Nor Pray'rs without success.

16 God by his Judgments do's declare
  His righteousness to all:
  They that lay Trains to hurt the good,
  Set Traps for their own fall.

17 Yea Hell their ruine waits, who God
  And Justice disregard:
18 When poor mens wronged Patience
  Shall find a sure reward.

19 Arise O Lord, and overturn
  The wickeds good success:
20 Affrigth them so, that they may know
  They're men, and so confess.

Psalm XI.

1 I Trust in God, why should I then
  By those discourag'd be,

Who

Who bid me like a frighted Bird
   Unto the Mountains flee?
2 For crafty Foes my ruine wait,
   Have ready bent their bow:
3 If the Foundations be destroy'd,
   What can the righteous do?

4 God in his Sanctuary dwells,
   Heav'n is his glorious Throne;
From whence he views the Sons of Men,
   And judges every one,
5 When he examines righteous men,
   He do's their works approve;
Such as are wicked and unjust,
   His Soul can lever love.

6 Snares shall befall them, and for these
   This mixture is made up,
Fire, Brimstone, and tempestuous storms,
   The portion of their Cup.
7 God, who himself is righteous, do's
   In righteousness delight;
And still will favour and protect
   The man that is upright.

Psalm XII.

(As the 100 *Psalm.)*

1 IF thou, Lord, dost not rise and help,
   Goodness from Earth will fly away;
And faithfull men will hardly find
A place, if thou much longer stay.

2 Dis-

2 Diſſimulation credit gains,
   They're counted wiſe that act a part;
   Who tho' their words are ſmooth and fair,
   Intend no kindneſs in their heart.

3 God will baſe Flatterers deſtroy,
   And their deceitfull arts will ſhame;
   Whoſe Pride no vengeance fears from God,
   And count Religion but a name.

4 Pow'r is their Juſtice; whoſe defects
   By fraud and falſhood they ſupply;
   And plead for their injurious tongues
   And uncontrolled Liberty.

5 But God who hears the poor mans ſighs,
   And groans of ſuch as are oppreſt;
   At length will vindicate their cauſe,
   And raiſe his Pow'r to give them reſt.

6 Gods words from all deceit are pure,
   His faithfulneſs has oft been try'd;
   Refined Silver's not ſo free
   From droſs, tho' ſeven times purifyd.

7 Thy promiſes ſhall never fail;
   Thou Lord ſhalt keep the juſt from harm;
8 Tho' when the vileſt men have pow'r,
   The wicked every where will ſwarm,

Pſalm XII

(Another Metre.)

1 Lord, if thou doſt not come and help,
   Goodneſs will fly away:

And

And faithfull men will find no place,
    If thou much longer stay.
2 Diſſimulation credit gains,
    They're wiſe that act a part:
Who tho' their words are ſmooth, intend
    No kindneſs in their heart.

3 God will baſe Flatterers deſtroy,
    And all their Arts will ſhame;
Who fear not Gods Revenge. and count
    Religion but a name.
4 Pow'r is their Juſtice; whoſe defects
    By falſhood they ſupply ;
And plead for their injurious tongues
    Unbounded Liberty.

5 But God that hears the ſighs and groans
    Of ſuch as are oppreſt ;
Will vindicate their cauſe, and raiſe
    His pow'r to give them reſt.
6 Gods words from all deceit are free,
    His Truth has oft been try'd ;
Silver is not ſo free from droſs,
    Tho' ſeven times purify'd.

7 Thy promiſe, Lord, ſhal never fail
    To keep the juſt from harm;
8 Tho', when the vile have pow'r, bad men
    On every ſide will ſwarm.

                            Pſalm

Psalm XIV.

(*As the* 100 *Psalm.*)

1 THe Fools believe there is no God
   That minds th' affairs of men below:
For tho' they speak it not aloud,
They live as if they thought it so.

Their principles are all corrupt,
Hatefull and vile their action are;
They're onely skilfull to do ill,
But from all good estranged far.

2 God from his glorious Throne above,
Look'd down and took a strict survey,
What men did seek and know the Lord,
And did his just Commands obey.

3 He found them all degenerate,
With loathsome wickedness o'ergrown;
None were Religious and Just,
Or practis'd goodness, no not one.

4 'Tis strange, they should without remorse
Like bread thy people thus devour;
Yet neither own thee by their Prayr'ts,
Nor dread the vengeance of thy pow'r.

5 For all their confidence and pride,
Terrors shall seize them unawares;
When God appears to help the just,
And Punishment for these prepares.

6 You now deride their trust in God;
7 But when from bondage he shal bring

Sal-

Salvation to his people; then
You fhal be fad and they fhall fing.

Pfalm XIV.

(*Another Metre.*)

1 FOols in their hearts have faid, No God
        Do's mind th' affairs below;
For tho' they fpeak it not aloud,
        They live as if' twere fo.
Their principles are all corrupt,
        Their actions hatefull are;
They're skilfull onely to do ill,
        From good eftranged far.

2 God from his Throne above look'd down,
        And took a ftrict furvey,
What men did feek and know the Lord,
        And his juft Laws obey.
3 He found them all degenerate,
        With loathfome fins o'ergrown;
What was Religious, juft and good,
        None practis'd, no not one.

4 Strange! that they fhould without remorfe,
        Like Bread the poor devour:
Yet neither own thee by their Pray'rs,
        Nor dread thy mighty pow'r.
5 For all their confidence, ftrange fears
        Shal Seize them unawares;
When God do's help the juft, for thefe
        Due vengeance he prepares.

6 Yoy.

You now deride their truſt in God,
　But when his pow'r ſhal bring
Salvation to his people, then
　You'll ſigh, and they ſhall ſing.

Pſalm XV.

L Ord let me know that happy man,
　Whom thou ſo well doſt love;
That he may praiſe thee here below,
　And dwell with thee above.
'Tis he, whoſe life is free from blame,
　Whoſe works are right and juſt;
Whoſe heart and words are true, and whom
　One may ſecurely truſt.

His Neighbours credit do's not wound
　By a detracting tongue:
Nor in his Infamy delights;
　Much leſs would do him wrong.
Vile men and their lewd practices,
　His vertuous Soul do's loath;
But ſhews to ſuch as fear the Lord,
　Kindneſs and honour both.

Who do's not break his Oath, when he
　To his own damage ſwears;
But his ſtrict vertue far before
　His intereſt prefers.
Who hates exaction, and rejects
　Bribes to betray the juſt:
This man ſhall ne'er be mov'd but may
　In God ſecurely truſt.

Pſalm

Psalm XVI.

5 GOD is my Portion, all my good
From his rich mercy flows ;
And his good Providence secures
The blessings he bestows.
6 I envy not the great mans state,
Nor pine to see his store :
With what I have I'm pleased much,
With what I hope for more.

7 I'll bless the Lord, ev'n when he makes
Troubles mine exercise ;
Those sad and solitary thoughts
Instruct and make me wise.
8 When God is present to my mind,
My fears are over-blown ;
When he stands by me with his aid,
No pow'r shall cast me down.

9 Therefore my heart and tongue rejoice,
In him my Flesh shall trust ;
10 My Soul shall not remain in Hell,
Nor Body in the Dust.
11 The path of life they both shall find ;
And in thy presence tast
Pleasures to full perfection grown,
And joys that ever last.

Psalm XIX.

1 THE Heav'ns, whose beauteous frame we
Gods Skill and Pow'r proclaim ;   (see,
2 The

2 The Laws by which each Day succeeds
    The Night, declare the same.
3 These tho' they have no voice like ours,
    Nor words to them belong ;
4 Yet these express to all the World
    Thy praise, without a tongue.

5 The Sun has there a glorious Tent :
    No Bridegroom shews his Face
So chearfull, nor no Champion runs
    With so much strength his Race.
6 Forth from the Eastern Coast he bends
    His course unto the West :
All th' Earth rejoices in his light,
    And by his heat is blest.

7 Gods Law's a perfect Rule of Life,
    Our errours this discries ;
Sinners to goodness this converts,
    And makes the simple wise.
8 To Reason and our better Pow'rs
    His just Commands accord :
Their joys are pure, and to the Soul
    Both Food and Light afford.

Part. II.

9 Thy fear, O Lord, can cleanse our Souls,
    And keep them pure and bright :
Thy Judgments are exactly true,
    And altogether right.
10 More to be prised than treasures, which
    With finest Gold are fill'd :

B   Swee-

Sweeter than Honey, and the drops
From Honey-Combs distill'd.

11 These are my Monitors, to whom
My prosperous state I own:
And in observing these shall gain
Rewards that are unknown.
12 But all the failings of his life
What man can call to mind?
Lord, let those faults thy pity move,
And easie pardon find.

13 Tho' frail I am, let no bold crimes
Enslave my Soul to sin:
So shall I blameless innocence
Maintain, and peace within.
14 My Pray'rs and praises then shall be
A pleasing Sacrifice
To thee, my God, in whom my strength
And my Salvation lies.

Psalm XXI.

1 O Lord, how joyfull is the King
With thy Salvation blest!
2 Thou'st given him his hearts desire,
And granted his request.
3 Prevented by thy wond'rous Love
A splendid Crown he wears;
4 The Life he asked was prolong'd
T'innumerable years.

5 By thee preferv'd, his Glory's great,
   With Majefty array'd;
6 By thee for ever highly bleft,
   And in thy favour glad.
7 The King do's on the Lord rely,
   Whofe grace will make him ftand:
8 But thofe that are thy Foes, fhall know
   The Terrour of thy hand.

9 Thy flaming wrath fhall them devour,
10   And all their Seed root out:
11 Repay the mifchief they defign'd,
   But could not bring about.
12 Thefe fhall be made the mark, at which
   Thy killing Arrows aim;
13 Thus, Lord, exalt thy Pow'r, and we
   Will fing, and praife thy Name.

Pfalm XXII.

25 THe praifes due to thee, O Lord,
   Shall in thy Church be pay'd;
Before thy Saints thofe vows perform'd,
   That in diftrefs I made.
26 The longings of the poor and meek
   Thy goodnefs fhall fupply:
Thou fhalt revive their fainting hopes,
   That on thy ftrength rely.

27 The Gentiles by his Kindnefs won,
   Shall turn unto the Lord;

B 2   By

By all the Kindreds of the Earth
   His name shall be ador'd.
28 The Lord is King; and under him
   Princes their Scepters sway;
All Nations pay him homage, and
   His pow'rfull Rule obey.

29 The Rich with plenty fill'd, the Poor
   That wallow in the Dust;
Both shall adore, and thee alone
   Their great Preserver trust.
30 A chosen Seed shall to their Race
   Declare his Righteousness:
31 What God has done for them, will raise
   His Mercies fame no less.

Psalm XXIII.

(As the 100 Psalm.)

1 GOD is my Shepherd, who will see
      That all my wants be still supply'd;
I shall not be expos'd to wrong,
Nor left to stray without a Guide.

2 The Pastures they are fresh and green,
Where I have ease and sweet repast:
The streams are cool and quiet, where
I quench my thirst and please my tast.

3 His comforts, which revive my Soul,
Lifes tedious journey pleasant make;
And in the peacefull ways of grace
He leads me, for his goodness sake.

4 Tho' I should walk, where black despair,
And sorrow casts a dismal shade;

                                    4 Thy

Thy Power and thy tender care
Would chase my fears, and make me glad.

5 Thou spread'st my Table, where my Foes
Behold thy Bounty, and repine
To see rich Oils anoint my head,
And see my Cup o'erflow with Wine.

6 Surely the Goodness of the Lord
Shall still surround me all my days:
I will frequent thy House, and there
Display thy Love, and sing thy praise.

Psalm XXIII.

(*Another Metre.*)

1 THE Lord my carefull Shepherd is,
I to his flock belong:
I shall not stray without a Guide,
Nor be expos'd to wrong.

2 The pastures they are fresh and green,
Where I have food and ease:
He leads me to the quiet streams
Where I my thirst appease.

3 His comforts which refresh my Soul,
Lifes journey pleasant make:
He guides me in his righteous paths,
For his own Goodness sake.

4 Tho' I should walk where black despair
Reflects a dismal shade;
Thy Rod and Staff would chase away
My fears, and make me glad.

5 In presence of my Foes, thou spread'st
My Table, who repine

To see rich Oils anoint my Head,
    My Cup o'erflow with Wine.
6. Surely the Goodness of the Lord
    Shall Crown my future days;
   I will frequent his House, to shew
    His Love, and sing his praise.

Psalm XXIV.

1 THE Earth's the Lords, to him belong
    All Creatures it contains;
His gratious care to all the World
    Extends, o'er which he Reigns.

2 He did upon the floating Seas
    The Earths great Fabrick lay;
And on th'unstable Floods, he made
    Her fixt Foundations stay.

3 Into that Hill where God resides,
    Who shall admitted be?
Lord, who within thy holy place,
    May stand and worship thee?

4 He whose unspotted hands no crimes,
    Whose heart no stains defile;
Whose tongue blasphemes not God nor
    His Neighbour to beguile   (swears

5 Such men unto thine Altar may
    Their free approaches make;
God hears their Pray'rs, and they are sure
    His Blessings to partake.

7 Ye Gates and everlasting Doors,
    Be open and make room;

Lift

Lift up your Heads, and you shall see
   The King of Glory come.
8 If you demand, what Lord is this?
   And who's this Glorious King?
It is the Mighty Lord of Hosts,
   Who do's Salvation bring.

Psalm XXV.

1 TO God I make my Pray'r,
   In him my trust repose;
2 O let me not become a scorn
   Or triumph to my Foes,
3 Let no Events deject
   Their Souls that wait on thee:
Let disappointments shame their hopes,
   That deal perfidiously.

4 The ways thou, Lord, dost chuse
   Make me to know aright:
And teach me always to perform
   What's pleasing in thy sight.
5 From the streight paths of Truth
   Ne'er let me go astray;
From thee, my Saviour, I beg
   Direction every day.

6 Lord, call to mind that Love,
   Thou didst of old express;
How thou hast gratiously reliev'd
   Thy Servants, in distress.
7 Into my youthfull sins
   No strict inquiry make:

B 4

Those

Thoſe early faults, O Lord, forgive,
For thine own goodneſs ſake.

Part. II.

8 God who is good and juſt,
   Will erring Souls inſtruct;
   Their wandring ſteps to the ſafe paths
   Of Vertue will conduct.
9 The humble Souls he'll guide,
   And teach the meek his way;
10 Kindneſs and Truth expreſs to ſuch
   As his juſt Laws obey.

11 Incourag'd by thy grace,
   For mercy I intreat;
   Pardon my Sins, O Lord, that are
   Both numerous and great.
12 Who is that happy Man
   That fears the Lord above?
   He'll ever lead him in the ways
   That he himſelf doth love.

13 Poſſeſs'd with quiet thoughts
   His Soul ſhall dwell at eaſe;
   His Seed ſhall after him enjoy
   Proſperity and Peace.
14 The ſecrets of his Love
   God will make known to thoſe
   That fear him, and the bleſſings he
   Reſerves, to them diſcloſe.

Part. III.

15 In all my troubles, Lord,
   Mine Eyes are towards thee;

I ho-

I hope thy goodneſs at the laſt
From all will ſet me free.
16 Lord, turn a gratious Eye
To me, and mercy ſhow;
Great are th' afflictions I endure,
And find no help below.

17 My troubles are enlarg'd,
Lord, ſend me quick relief;
18 Grant me forgiveneſs of my ſins,
And then remove my grief.
19 Conſider how my Foes
In Number ſtill increaſe;
How they with cauſeleſs hatred ſeek
The ruine of my Peace.

20 Preſerve and keep my Soul
From ſhame as well as guilt;
O never diſappoint the hopes
That I on thee have built.
21 Let my try'd Innocence
Find ſure ſupports from thee;
At length thy choſen people, Lord,
From all their troubles free.

Pſalm XXVI.

1 PLead thou my cauſe, O thou that know'ſt
My Souls integrity:
Nothing ſhal ſhake my Confidence,
Whilſt I on thee rely.
2 Mine inmoſt thoughts I offer, Lord,
To thine impartial Eye;

B 5   O try

O try my heart, left any fin
   Should there concealed lie.

5 The contemplation of thy Love
   Gives me the beft delight:
  This both engages and excites
   My care to walk aright.

6 My thoughts and actions I'll preferve
   Free from impurity;
  And then th' Oblations I prefent,
   Shall acceptable be.

7 Then I aloud with chearfull voice
   Thy goodnefs will proclaim;
  And tell of all thy wond'rous works,
   To magnify thy Name.

Pfalm XXVII.

7 TO my Petitions, Lord, return
   An anfwer full of grace:
8 Thy face thou bad'ft me feek, and I
   Refolve to feek thy face.

9 Lord, do not in difpleafure hide
   Thy face, nor me reject;
  Thofe fuccours I have had before,
   From thee I ftill expect.

10 My Parents Love is not fo great
   As thine, nor care fo large;
  When they forfake me, I become
   Still more thy care and charge.

11 Lord, let me plainly fee the way
   Where I may fafely tread;

Avoi-

Avoiding all the cunning snares
   Mine Enemies have laid.

13 How wretched had I been, when I
   With troubles was opprest,
Had I not hop'd thy mercy would
   Secure my Peace and Rest.
14 Wait still on God, my Soul, from him,
   Courage and Strength derive;
Tho' he delay, he will at length
   Thy fainting heart revive.

Psalm XXVIII.

1 HEar me, O Lord, my sure defence,
   When I thy succour crave;
Else I shall be like them that lie
   Neglected in the Grave.
6 Blest be the Lord, who bow'd his Ear
   To those requests I made;
7 I trusted in his strength and found
   His seasonable aid.

Thy favour, Lord, has made my heart
   Exceedingly rejoice;
In gratefull Hymns I will advance
   Thy praise with chearfull voice.
8 Those that upon his Pow'r rely,
   God will protect and own;
And his Anointed save whom he
   Has raised to his Throne:
9 Lord, bless thy people, who to thee
   Do all their safety owe;
Feed thou thy Flock, and raise them up
   When they are fallen low.

Psalm

Psalm XXIX.

(*As the* 100 *Psalm.*)

1 THE glorious Empire of the Lord
   Ye Rulers of the World proclaim;
2 And in his Sanctuary give
   The Honour due unto his Name.

3 Heark, how his thund'ring voice do's run
   Through all the Regions of the Sky;
   The Clouds are frighted with the noise,
4 So full of Pow'r and Majesty.

5 The lofty Cedars bow their Heads,
   And break before the mighty sound;
6 Mountains that bear them feel the shock,
   And like a frighted Calf rebound.

7 Before this voice the dreadfull flames
   Of pointed Lightnings tear the air,
8 Wild Creatures, that in desarts dwel,
   Think they're not safe, but quake for fear.

9 This makes the timorous Hinds to Calve,
   Wild Beasts the naked Thickets leave;
   But in his sacred Temple all
   Fearless to God their praises give.

10 The Lords Dominion do's extend
   To Clouds above and Floods below;
11 This great Protector of the good,
   Will rest and Peace on his bestow.

Psalm

Pfalm XXX.

(As the 100 Pfalm.)

MY God, fince thou haft rais'd me up,
    Thee I'll extoll with thankfull voice;
Who haft fecur'd me from thofe harms,
That would have made my Foes rejoyce.

2 With troubles worn, and grief opprefs'd,
  To thee I cry'd, and thou didft fave;
3 Thou didft fupport my finking hopes,
  My Life didft refcue from the Grave.

4 Wherefore rejoice ye Saints of his,
  Proclaim the praifes of the Lord;
His goodnefs often call to mind,
  And his Fidelity record.

5 His anger is but fhort; his Love,
  Which is our Life, do's longer ftay;
Grief may continue for a night,
  But comfort rifes with the day.

11 By thee my mournfull ftate is chang'd,
  My Sackloth now is thrown away;
And gladnefs girds me who before
  In black defpair and horrour lay.

12 My tongue no longer filent be,
  But to the Lord due glory give;
And ftrive that in thy thankfull Verfe
  His fame Eternally may live.

Pfalm

Pſalm XXX.
(*Another Metre.*)

1 SInce thou haſt rais'd me, I'll extoll
  My God with thankfull voice;
  Who free'd me from thoſe harms, that
  Have made my Foes rejoice.   (would

2 With grief and troubles worn, to thee
  I cry'd and thou did'ſt ſave:

3 Thou, Lord, my ſinking hopes and life
  Didſt reſcue from the Grave.

4 Then let the Saints with joy proclaim
  The praiſes of the Lord;
  His goodneſs call to mind: and his
  Fidelity record.

5 His wrath's but ſhort: his Love, which is
  Our Life, do's longer ſtay:
  Weeping may for a Night endure,
  But joy comes with the Day.

11 My mournſull State is chang'd, and now
  My Sackcloth's thrown away;
  Gladneſs ſurrounds me, who before
  In diſmal ſorrows lay.

12 My Tongue no longer ſilent be;
  To God due praiſes give;
  That in thy thankfull verſe, his fame
  Eternally may Live.

Pſalm XXXII.
(*As the* 100 *Pſalm.*)

1 OHappy Man! whom God forgives
  And hides what he has done amiſs;
                                    2 Owns

2 Owns him as if he had not sinn'd,
  Whose heart sincere and upright is:
3 My woes increas'd, whilst I supprest
  My guilt, no quiet I could get;
4 Thy wrath did press me like a weight,
  And scorch'd me like the Summers heat.
5 I then resolved to disclose
  My crimes, and open all my wound;
  I humbly did confess my sins
  To thee, and easie pardon found.
6 This mercy shall invite good men
  In season to implore thine aid;
  Then tho' their troubles like a Flood
  Should rise, they need not be afraid.
7 Thou, Lord, shalt be my safe retreat,
  To thee I'll fly in all distress;
  Thou wilt preserve me; and in Songs
  Of Victory I'll thee confess.
8 I'll counsel Sinners to obey;
9 And not be like the Horse or Mule,
  Whose fury, till they're broke and tam'd,
  No Rein can guide, no Curb can rule.
10 Such Sinners meet with heavy strokes;
11 While those that trust in God, shall prove
  The happy men; then let the Just
  Rejoice and triumph in his Love.

Psalm XXXII.
(*Another Metre*)

2 O Blessed man whom God forgives,
    And hides what's done amiss: 2 On

2 On whom no ſin is charg'd; whoſe heart
   Sincere and upright is.

3 Whilſt I ſuppreſs'd my inward guilt,
   No quiet I could get:

4 Thy hand did preſs me, and thy wrath
   Scorch'd me like Summers heat.

5 I then reſolved to diſcloſe
    My Crimes, and ope' my wound:
I humbly did confeſs my ſins,
    And eaſie pardon found,

6 This mercy ſhall in ſeaſon draw
   Good men t'implore thy aid :
Then tho' the Floods of Trouble riſe,
   They need not be afraid.

7 Thou art my Refuge, Lord, to thee
   I'll fly in all diſtreſs ;
Thou wilt preſerve me; and my Songs
   Thy mercies ſhal confeſs.

8 I'll teach proud men t'obey; and not
   Be like the Horſe or Mule ;

9 Whoſe fury till they're broke, no Rein
   Can guide, no Curb can rule.

10 Such meet with heavy ſtrokes; whilſt thoſe
   That truſt in God, ſhall prove
The happy men: then let them joy
   And Triumph in his Love.

Pſalm XXXIII.

(As the 100 *Pſalm.)*

1 YE righteous in the Lord rejoice,
   And let his praiſe be your delight;
                    For

For praise is lovely, and becomes
The lips of those that are upright.

4 Gods word is, like its Author, good,
His Laws from all injustice free;
His promise sure, and all his works
Are done in Truth and Equity.

5 Works that are right and just, secure
His favour, and his pleasure are;
The Earth with various blessings fill'd,
To us his kindness do's declare.

6 The vast extended Orbs of Heav'n
By his commanding word were made;
And all its numerous Hosts, from his
Creating breath their beings had.

7 The Seas proud Waves within the shores,
To which they are confined, keep;
Whose Waters safely are laid up
In the great Store-House of the deep.

8 Then to the Lord by men on Earth
Let fear and due regard be shown;
May all the World his awfull pow'r
By humble adorations own.

Part. II.

12 O happy he! whose service shows
That God his chosen Ruler is;
And happy they! whom God declares
By's special care, that they are his.

13 Th'Almighty on the Sons of Men
Looks down from his Celestial Throne;
C
14

14 And all the dwellers on the Earth
   Views from his glorious Mansion.

15 He equally did make them all,
   Their hearts he fashion'd one by one;
   And all their inmost thoughts, to him
   Better than to themselves, are known.

18 The Lord on those that fear his Name
   Looks with a favourable Eye;
   He ne'er will fail their hopes, that on
   His goodness stedfastly rely.

20 Now, Lord, we wait for thee, thou art
   Our succour and our sure defence;
21 What e'er befalls us, we may trust
   In thee with chearfull confidence.

22 So let thy mercies, Lord, on us
   Descend, like a refreshing show'r;
   As all our hope and joy depends
   Upon thy favour and thy pow'r.

Psalm XXXIII.
(Another Metre.)

1 REjoyce, ye Righteous, in the Lord,
      And praise him with delight:
   For thankfulness becomes the lips
      Of those that are upright.
4 His word is good, and all his Laws
      Are from injustice free;
   His promise sure; and all his ways
      Are Truth and Equity.

5 Works

5 Works that are juſt ſecure his Love,
 As they his pleaſure are;
The Earth with bleſſings fill'd, to us
 His goodneſs do's declare.
6 Th' extended Orbs of Heav'n, by his
 Commanding word were made;
And from his Breath its numerous Hoſts
 Their ſeveral Beings had.

7 The Seas proud Waves within the ſhores
 Confined limits keep;
Whoſe waters are laid up within
 The Storehouſe of the deep.
8 Let all men fear the Lord, to him
 Let due regard be ſhown:
May all the World his awfull pow'r
 By humble worſhip own.

Part. II.

12 O happy he! whoſe ſervice ſhows
 That God his Ruler is;
And happy they! whom God declares
 By's Care, that they are his.
13 God on the Sons of Men looks down
 From his Celeſtial Throne;
14 Views all the dwellers on the Earth
 From his bright Manſion.

15 He made them equally, their hearts
 He Faſhion'd one by one;
More clearly all their thoughts to him,
 Than to themſelves are known.

18 The Lord on those that fear his Name
    Looks with a Gratious Eye:
    And ne'er will fail their hopes, that on
    His Goodness do rely.

20 Now, Lord, we wait for thee, who art
    Our help and our defence:
21 In all Estates we trust in thee
    With chearfull confidence.
22 Lord, let thy grace on us descend
    Like a refreshing show'r;
    For all our hope and joys depend
    On thine Almighty Pow'r.

Psalm XXXIV.

1 GOD, who my kind Preserver is,
    I will at all times bless;
    My tongue shall daily be employ'd
    His goodness to confess.
2 In God my Soul shall boast, good men
    Shall hear it, and rejoice;
3 And to exalt his glorious Name,
    Join both in heart and voice.

4 I sought the Lord in my distress,
    And graciously he heard,
    His timely succours did prevent
    The threatning harm I fear'd.
7 Blest Angels, which on God attend,
    Yet wait t'encompass such
    As fear him, to preserve them safe
    When dangers near approach.

8 O taste and see, as I have done;
 And then confess you must,
That God is good, and they are blest
 That in his goodness trust.

Part. II.

12 What man would have his years prolong'd
 And happy days would see?
13 Refrain thy tongue and lips from all
 Deceit and Injury.
14 From all unrighteous ways depart,
 From doing good ne'er cease ;
Seek all mens quiet, and pursue
 The things that make for peace.

15 God loves the righteous, and on them
 He casts a gratious Eye ;
His Ear's attentive to their suits
 And open to their cry.
17 Nor do they cry in vain: wish'd help
 And ease their troubles have ;
18 God will draw near to broken hearts,
 And contrite spirits save.

19 Tho' good men oft afflicted are,
 At lenght God sets them free ;
20 His care do's to their Bodies reach,
 No bone shall broken be
21 Bad men shall perish, when they're plagu'd,
 With all that hate the Just ;
22 Whom God will keep, and never fail
 Their hopes that on him trust.

C 3

Pſalm XXXVI.

5 BEyond the limits of the Skie
  Thy mercy, Lord, extends;
Thy faithfulneſs the narrow bounds
  Of ſpace and time tranſcends.
6 Mountains may be remov'd, before
  Thy truth ſhall fail the leaſt;
Thy judgments none can fathom; thou
  Preſerveſt Man and Beaſt.

7 But who can prize enough that Love
  God bears unto the juſt;
Under whoſe Providence and care
  Good men ſecurely truſt.
8 They to the Plenty of thy Houſe
  For all ſupplies ſhall look;
And freely of thy pleaſures drink
  As from a running Brook.

9 For all the Springs of Joy and Life
  Derived are from thee;
From thy continued favour flows
  All our Felicity.
10 To thoſe that thus eſteem thy Love,
  Thy kindneſs ſtill impart;
And all thy promiſes fulfill
  To men of upright heart.

Pſalm XXXVII.

(As the 100 *Pſalm.)*

1 LEt none be envious, when he ſees
  The wickeds proſperous Eſtate;

Nor

Nor, tempted by their good success,
Grow bold their Crimes to imitate.

2 For so the Grass is fresh and green,
Before the Mower cuts it down;
And beauteous Flow'rs, within a while
Are withered by the scorching Sun.

3 He's wise that's always doing good,
And on God's goodness do's rely;
4 Thus thy Enjoyments he'll secure,
And all thy just desires supply.

5 Leave thy concerns unto his care,
In firm dependance on him live;
He'll either grant what thou wouldst have,
Or, what he knows is better, give.

6 Tho' slanders and detracting tongues,
Like Clouds, thy Righteousness obscure;
He"ll clear thy Innocence, the Light
At Noon shall not appear more pure.

16 Think not mere wealth makes happy men;
That little which contents the poor,
Is better far, than wicked mens
Ill-got or ill-employed store.

Part. II.

23 The Lord directs a good man's steps
And he delighteth in his way;
24 He is not ruin'd by his falls,
God's pow'r is his support and stay.

25 In all th' experience of my life,
That Liberal man I ne'er could see,

C 4

Who.

Whose Alms expos'd himself to want,
Or brought his Race to Beggary.

26. He's ever mercifull and lends,
And thus his Seed a blessing gain;

27 If thou wouldst therefore happy be,
Do good and from all sin abstain.

28 For God whose Nature's good and just,
Those that are like himself will own;
They shall continue; when the race
Of wicked men is overthrown.

35 I've seen the wicked rise to pow'r,
Flourish like Laurels ever green;

36 But suddenly their ruine came,
And no remainder could be seen.

37 Mark but the good and perfect man,
And him that's upright in his ways;
Mercy attends his happy life,
And quiet peace concludes his days.

Psalm XXXVII.

(*Another Metre*.)

1 LEt none be troubled to behold
The wickeds prosp'rous State;
Nor by their good success grow bold
Their crimes to imitate.

2 For Grass is fresh and green, before
The Mower cuts it down;
And beauteous Flowers within, a while
Are withered by the Sun.

3 He's wise that's doing good, and on
 God's goodness do's rely;
4 Thus thy Enjoyments he'll secure,
 Thy just desires supply.
5 Leave thy concerns to him, in firm
 Dependance on him live;
He'll either grant what thou would'st have,
 Or what is better give.

6 Tho' slanderous tongues should like a
 Thy Righteousness obscure; (Cloud
He'll clear thy innocence, the light
 Shall not appear more pure.
16 Think not mere wealth makes happy men;
 For what contents the poor,
Is better than Bad mens Ill-got.
 Or ill'employed store,

Part. II.

23 The Lord that guides a good man's steps,
 Delighteth in his way;
24 He is not ruin'd by his falls,
 God's pow'r will be his stay.
25 In all my Life I never yet
 That liberal man could see;
Whose Alms expos'd himself to want,
 Or Race to Beggary.

26 He mercifully lends and thus
 His Seed a blessing gain;
27 If thou wouldst then be blest, do good
 And from all sin abstain.

28 God that is Good and Juſt, will thoſe
    That him reſemble own;
  They ſhall continue, when the Race
    Of Bad men is o'erthrown.

35 I've ſeen the wicked riſe, and ſpread
    Like Laurels freſh and green;
36 But when his haſty ruine came,
    No remnant could be ſeen.
37 Mark but the perfect man, and him
    That's upright in his ways;
  Mercy attends his happy life,
    And peace concludes his days.

Pſalm XXXIX.

(As the 100 Pſalm.)

4 Lord, teach me, when my latter end
    And number of my days I view;
  To meaſure right my ſelf and them,
  How I am frail, and they are few.

5 My days extent is but a ſpan,
  Mine age is nothing unto thee;
  Man in his flouriſhing eſtate
  Is altogether vanity.

6 A ſhadow's all that he purſues;
  But his vexations real are;
  He heaps up wealth, and knows not who
  Shall reap the profit of his care.

7 Let others Fooliſhly expect
  How kind the flatt'ring World will prove;
                       I'll

I'll seek my God alone to please,
And be ambitious of his Love,

11 How weak and nothing we appear,
When God for sin do's man chastise!
Like Garments fretted by the moth,
So all his beauty ruin'd lies.

12 My poor Petitions, Lord, regard,
And to my mournfull cry give Ear;
A wandring stranger here on Earth
I am, as all my Fathers were.

13 Lord, my decaying strength repair,
And spare me yet a while, that I
May make my peace with thee, before
I go away from hence and dye.

Psalm XXXIX.

(*Another Metre.*)

4 LOrd, teach me, when my end and days
I have to live, I view;
To know my self and them, how frail
I am, and they are few.

5 My days are but a span, mine Age
Is nothing unto thee;
When man is in his best estate,
He's onely vanity.

6 A shadow he pursues, but his
Vexations real are;
Gets wealth, but knows not who shall reap
The profit of his care.

7 Let

7 Let others foolishly expect
      How kind the World will prove;
   I'll seek to please my God, and be
      Ambitious of his Love.

11 How weak alas! we are, when God
      For sin do's Man chastise;
   Like Garments fretted by the moth,
      His Beauty ruin'd lies.

12 My mournfull State, O Lord, regard,
      And to my cry give Ear;
   I am a stranger here on Earth,
      As all my Fathers were.

13 Repair my strenght, O God, and spare
      Me yet a while, that I
   May make my peace with thee, before
      I go from hence, and dye.

Psalm XL.

1 'TIS good with patience to attend,
      And on the Lord rely;
   When other Succours fail'd, to him
      I pray'd, who heard my cry.

2 I that in misery was plung'd,
      Surrounded with despair,
   Am safely plac'd above my fears,
      And firm my goings are.

3 And now I'll chearfull praises sing
      To God, that set me free;
   Whilst this thy goodness do's invite
      Others to trust in thee.

4 O happy man that trusts in God,
   And can the proud despise!
With the deceitfull arts of such
   As turn aside to lies.

Part. II.

5 Thy wond'rous works and thoughts of Lo-
   To us so many are;   (ve
If I would tell them, they exceed
   My thoughts and value far.
When Sacrifices, Lord, to thee
   No longer gratefull were;
And when obedience thou before
   Burnt Offerings didst prefer.

7 Instead of these, that I should come,
   Thy Sacred Books recite;
8 Thy Law is in my heart, and I
   To do thy will delight.

9 Within thy Church I have made known
   How great thy Mercies are;
Thy Truth and Faitfulness, my tongue
   To publish shall not spare.

11 O let my preservation speak
   How true thou art and kind;
And those compassions I proclaim,
   Lord, let me ever find.

Psalm XLI.

(As the 100 Psalm.)

1 BLest is the man, whose tender sense
   Is touched with another's grief;

Who

Who when he hears the poor man's cry,
Affords him pity and relief.

God will his Charity repay,
In time of need will be his Friend;
When troubles to his Lot shall fall,
He'll make them have an happy end.

2 Threatned by danger or disease,
His Life he'll rescue from the Grave;
Prosper his State on Earth; and from
His Foes and all their malice save.

3 He'll strengthen him upon his Bed
Of languishing infirmity;
Secure of God's compassions,
His weary Limbs will softer lie.

4 Wounded and sore opprest with guilt,
I cry'd for pity and for ease;
Lord, let thy mercies heal my Soul,
Whose sins are onely less than these.

13 Blest be that Majesty above,
Whom all true Worshippers adore;
Let every Age consent, and say
Amen, till time shall be no more.

Psalm XLII.

(As the 100 *Psalm.*)

1 O God, the Spring of all my joys,
For thee I long, to thee I look;
No chased Hart do's pant so much
After the cooling Water-brook.

2 Less grief it is to be exil'd
From mine own House, than, Lord, from
        thine;
Oh how I wisht t'approach that place,
Where all thy Glories use to shine.

3 The sorrows of my Banishment
Increase, and tears become my food;
Whilst mine insulting Foes reproach
My faith, and say, where's now thy God?

4 Past joys renew my Grief, to think
How to thine House in Troops we came;
What chearfull Feasts we kept, and sang
Praises in consort to thy Name.

5 Why should I cherish these sad thoughts
Whence nought but perturbation flows?
Since you procure not what I wish,
Why should you hinder my repose?

I've learnt the Remedy at last;
To keep my Passions calm and still;
I'm nearer help by hope in God.
And resignation to his will.

Psalm XLII.

(*Another metre.*)

BLest Fountain of my joys, for thee
   I long, to thee I look;
No chased Hart do's pant so much
   After the Water-brook.

2 Less grief it is to be exil'd
    From mine own House, than thine;
Oh how I wish t'approach the place,
    Where all thy Glories shine.

3 This makes my sorrows to increase,
    And tears become my food;
To hear my Foes reproach my Faith,
    And say, where's now thy God?

4 Past joys renew my Grief, to think
    How to thine House we came
In Troops to Feast, and praises sang
    In consort to thy Name.

5 Why should I cherish these sad thoughts
    Whence nought but trouble flows?
Since you procure not what I wish,
    Hinder not my repose,
I've learnt this Remedy, to keep
    My passions calm and still:
I'm nearer help by hope in God,
    And a resigned will.

Psalm XLIII.

(As the 100 Psalm.)

1 THou righteous Judge of all the World,
    Be thou my gracious Advocate;
And clear mine Innocence from those
    Whose craft is equal to their hate.

2 Why, Lord, dost thou with-hold that pow'r
    On which alone my Soul relies?

And

And look'st not on my mournfull state,
Opprest by cruel Enemies?

3 Thy mercy and thy truth display;
That by the conduct of thy Light
Thy Courts I may attain, and there
May have of thee a fuller sight.

4 T'approach thine Altar would revive
My Spirit, and all my gladness raise:
Where I thy goodness would proclaim
With all the Instruments of praise.

5 Why should I entertain sad thoughts
Whence nought but perturbation flows?
Since they procure not what I wish,
Why should they hinder my repose?

I've learnt this Remedy at last,
To keep my Passions calm and still;
I'm nearer help by hope in God,
And resignation to his will.

Psalm XLIII.

(Another Metre.)

1 GReat Judge of all the World, be thou
My gratious Advocate;
To plead my cause 'gainst those, whose craft
Is equal to their hate.

2 Why, Lord, dost thou with-hold that pow'r
On which my Soul relies?
And look'st not on my state oppress'd
By cruel Enemies?

D   3 Thy

3 Thy Mercy and thy Truth display,
     That, guided by thy Light,
I may attain thy Courts, and have
     Of thee a fuller fight.

4 T'approach thine Altar would revive
     My Soul, my joys would raise;
Where I thy goodness would proclaim
     With instruments of praise.

5 Why should I entertain sad thoughts,
     Whence nought but trouble flows?
Since you procure not what I wish,
     Hinder not my repose.

6 I've learnt this Remedy, to keep
     My passions calm and still;
I'm nearer help by hope in God,
     And a resigned will.

Psalm XLV.

(*As the* 100 *Psalm.*)

2 O Glorious King! thy form Divine
     Created Beauties do's outshine;
All graces on thy Lips are powr'd,
On thee Eternal Blessings showr'd.

3 Gird thy bright Sword upon thy thigh,
     The Ornament of Majesty;
Like an illustrious Prince appear,
And shew how great thy Glories are.

4 Ride on in triumph, and maintain
     The Vertues that adorn thy train;

                    Wrong'd

Wrong'd Meeknes, Truth and Equity
Look onely for support from thee.

Thine Enemies amazed stand,
Struck with the Terrour of thy hand;
5 Who needs must fall, since thy keen Darts
Will find a passage to their hearts.

6 Thy Throne, O God, is fixed sure,
Thy Kingdom ever shal endure;
Thy Laws, the Sceptre in thy hand,
Op, press not those whom they command.

7 Vice thou dost hate and Justice love;
Therefore thy Glories far above
Thy Fellows shine; thy God has shed
More Oil of Gladnes on thy head.

Psalm XLVI.

1 TH' Almighty Lord is our defence,
  The strength whereby we stand;
When troubles their approaches make,
  His help is nigh at hand.
2 Our faith may then remain unmov'd,
Tho' th' Earth should be displac'd;
Or tho' into the Seas vast gulph
  The Mountains should be cast.

3 Although the Oceans troubled waves
  A frightfull noise should be make;
Should rise and swel unto the Clouds,
  And cause the Hills to shake.

D 2

4 The.

4 There is a quiet stream makes glad
  The City of the Lord;
5 His presence will secure her peace,
  And timely help afford.

6 The Nations rage and threaten War,
  But God is on our side;
7 One word of his dissolves their force,
  And daunts their swelling pride.
8 See what his hand has done; it draws
  The Sword out of its sheath;
  Which, while he gives it leave, triumphs
  In slaughter and in death.

9 Then by another word he makes
  Destructive Wars to cease;
  He breaks their Arms, the Bow and Spear,
  And crowns the Earth with Peace.
10 Cease then, fond men, to strive with God,
  Whose pow'r is over all;
  For fear lest he exalt himself
  In your unpitied fall.

Psalm XLVII.

1 O All ye people, clap your hands,
    And make a chearfull noise;
  With Acclamations to your God
    Declare your inward joys.
2 His high Perfections do proclaim
    Him greatly to be fear'd;
  This King of all the World commands
    Your honour and regard.

5 In a triumphant state our Lord
    Is gone above the Skies;
Trumpets proclaim our joys, and all
    Applaud his Victories.

6 Sing chearfull praises to our God,
    Sing praises to our King;

7 He's Lord of all the Earth his praise
    With understandig sing.

8 God o'er the Heathen people reigns;
    And in that Throne is plac'd,
Where he in Glory sits, and thence
    Shall judge the World at last

Psalm XLIX.

(*As the* 100 *Psalm.*)

5 WHy should the Man that trusts in God,
    Affright himself with needless fear,
To see th' approaches of old Age,
Or that unwelcome Death draws near?

6 Vain men applaud their stores; yet none

7 His Brother can from dying save;

8 Lifes purchase is too great; no wealth

9 Can buy our freedom from the Grave

10 The Ashes of the wise and good
With Fools together mingled lye;
The rich, tho' loth to go, must leave
The World with all their wealth; and dye.

11 Some think on Houses that they build,
Their fame eternally shall stand;

D 3   And

  And, to preserve their memory,
  Give their own names unto their Land.

12 Death levels all their state with Beasts,
  Makes all their splendid Titles fade;
13 Yet their Posterity approves
  The Follies and mistakes they made.

14 Driv'n to theGrave likeSheep,their strength
  And Beauty shall consume away;
  And in Death's fold inclos'd shall lye;
  Till the great Resurrrection Day.

  A Day wherein the Just shall reign,
  And o'er the Bad Dominion have,
15 Then I shall be receiv'd to bliss,
  After I'm raised from the Grave,

Part. II.

16 Be not concern'd, when one's made rich,
  Or honour'd here; for when he dies,
17 Naked he goes away from hence,
  And stript of all his Glory lies.

18 Tho' whilst he liv'd he bless'd himself
  And other men are apt to praise
  His prudent management, that strives
  His Wealth or Family to raise;

19 It's Folly all; since he must tread
  The Path his Fathers went before;
  And in the place where now he dwells,
  Never see light or comfort more.

20 Man that to Honour is advanc'd,
And with true Wisedom is not blest,
Tho' pleas'd with false and flatt'ring hopes,
Shall die and perish like a Beast.

Psalm XLIX.

(*Another Metre*)

5 WHerefore should he that trusts in God,
Affright himself with fear,
To see old Age approach, or when
Unwelcome Death draws near?

6 Men boast their stores, and yet none can
7 From Death his Brother save;
8 Lifes purchase is too great, to buy
9 Our freedom from the Grave,

10 The Ashes of the wise, with Fools
Together blended lie;
The rich, tho' loth, must leave the World
With all their Wealth, and die.

11 Some think on Houses that they build
Their Fame shall ever stand;
And that their names may not be lost,
They give them to their Land.

12 Death levels all their pomp with Beasts;
Makes all their Titles fade;
13 Yet their Posterity approves
All the mistakes they made.

14 Driv'n to the Grave like Sheep, their
And Beauty fades away: (strength

And there fhall lie inclofed, till
   The Refurrection Day.
Then fhall the Juft men reign, and o'er
   The Bad Dominion have;
15 Then I fhall be receiv'd to Blifs,
   When raifed from the Grave.

Part. II.

16 Envy not him that's glorious here
   Or rich; for when he dies,
17 Naked he goes away, and ftript
   Of all his Glory lies.
18 Tho' whilft he liv'd he blefs'd himfelf;
   And men are apt to praife
   That prudent management, which wealth
   And Families do's raife;
19 'Tis Folly all; for he muft go
   Where others went before,
   And never, where he now muft dwell,
   See light or comfort more.
20 Man that is honour'd here, and with
   True wifedom is not bleft;
   Tho' pleas'd with flattering hopes, fhall die,
   And perifh like a Beaft.

Pfalm LI.

(As the 100 Pfalm.)

1 LOrd, look upon my finfull Soul,
   That unto thee for mercy flies;

As

As thy Compassions boundless are,
So blot out mine iniquities.

2 Oh wash me throughly from my crimes,
For thou alone canst make me clean:
3 With tears I now confess my guilt,
Amaz'd to see how vile I've been.

4 None else can call me to account;
But thy Tribunal, Lord, I fear;
For if arraign'd and judg'd by thee,
I must be cast, and thou be clear.

5 I was conceiv'd and born in sin,
Too prone and bent to do amiss;
6 But inward Purity to thee,
And truth of heart most pleasing is.

7 Lord, shew me thou art reconcil'd,
As those with Hyssop sprinkled know
They are absolv'd; thy Grace can wash
And make me whiter than the Snow.

8 My sins have forfeited the joys
And inward peace that once I had;
Thy pard'ning voice would heal again
My broken Bones, and make them glad

9 No longer, Lord, behold my sins
With a severe and angry look;
Oh take their stains out of my Soul,
And blot their guilt out of thy Book.

Part. II.

10 Create in me, O God, a heart
Clean and unspotted in thy sight;

Renew a well composed mind ;
Unmov'd from goodness, and upright.

11 Lord, do not cast me from thy sight,
As one whom thou no more canst love;
Nor let thy Spirit, whose grace I need,
Tho' griev'd too much, from me remove.

12 Its saving comforts and free aids,
T'uphold my feeble powr's, afford;
13 Thus Sinners will be drawn t'amend
Their ways, and turn unto the Lord.

14 Oh save me from the crying guilt
Of blood, that sin of Crimson dy;
I'll then thy faithfulness proclaim,
And loudly sing thy Clemency.

15 My opened lips shal speak thy praise;
16 For this thou rather dost desire
Than costly Sacrifice of Beasts,
Consumed wholly in the fire.

17 Thou, Lord, a broken contrite heart
Dost more than bloody off'rings prise;
This present now I humbly make,
Which God, I trust, will not despise.

Psalm LI.

(*Another Metre.*)

1 BEhold, O Lord, my sinfull Soul
To thee for Mercy flies;

Thy

Thy Mercy boundless is, blot out
    All mine iniquities.
2 Oh wash away my crimes, for thou
    Alone canst make me clean;
3 I now confess my guilt, amaz'd
    To see how vile I've been.

4 Tho' none can call me to account,
    Thy Sentence, Lord, I fear;
If judg'd by thee, I know I must
    Be cast, and thou be clear.
5 I was conceiv'd and born in sin,
    Too prone to do amiss;
6 But purity and truth of heart
    To thee most pleasing is.

7 Shew thou art reconcil'd, as those
    Whom Hyssop sprinkles know
They are absolv'd; thy Grace can wash,
    And make me white as snow.
8 My sins have forfeited the joys
    And peace that once I had;
Thy voice would heal my broken Bones,
    Thy Pardon make them glad.

9 No longer, Lord, behold my sins
    With a displeased look;
Oh take their stains out of my Soul,
    Their Guilt out of thy Book.

Part. II.

10 Create in me, O Lord, a heart
    Unspotted in thy sight;

Re-

Renew in me a mind unmov'd
From goodness, and upright.
11 Lord, do not cast me from thy sight,
As one thou canst not love;
Nor let thy Spirit, tho' griev'd too much,
Its grace from me remove'

12 Its comforts and free aids, t'uphold
My feeble pow'rs afford;
13 Thus Sinners will amend their ways,
And turn unto the Lord.
14 Oh save me from the guilt of blood,
That sin of Crimson dy;
Then I'll proclaim thy faithfulness,
And sing thy Clemency.

15 My opened lips shall speak thy praise;
For this thou dost desire
16 Rather than Sacrifice of Beasts,
Consumed in the Fire.
17 Thou dost a broken contrite heart
More than all off'rings prise;
This present now I humbly bring,
Which God will not despise.

Psalm LIII.

(As the 25 Psalm.)

1 THE Fools believe no God
Do's mind th'affairs below;
For tho' they speak it not aloud,
They live as if 'twere so.

AB

All are corrupt and vile,
 Their actions hatefull are;
They're onely skilfull to do ill,
 From good estranged far.

2 God from his Throne look'd down,
 And took a strict survey,
What men did seek and know the Lord,
 And his just Laws obey.

3 All were degenerate,
 With loathsome sins o'ergrown,
What was Religious, just and good,
 None practis'd, no not one.

4 Strange Madness! that they should
 Like Bread the poor devour;
And neither own thee by their Pray'rs,
 Nor dread thy mighty pow'r.

5 Where all their fears were vain,
Great terrours seis'd them there;
God that despis'd them made their fall
 As shamefull as their fear.

6 Lord, let thy peoples hopes
 Be with deliverance Crown'd;
When thy Salvation shall appear,
 Their joys shall then abound.

Psalm LVII.

1 Lord, since I trust in thee alone,
  Mercy to me extend;
I fly for shelter to thy Wings,
 Till all my troubles end.

2 To him whose Pow'r is over all,
    In my distress I'll cry;
    Since thou hast sav'd me heretofore,
    Thy help will still be nigh.

6 When with the Fowlers treacherous arts,
    My ruine was prepar'd;
    Their Pits occasion'd their own fall,
    Their Nets themselves insnar'd.
7 My heart, O God, is now prepar'd,
    And this my tongue shall raise;
8 Which with my Harp shall early sing
    A Consort to thy praise.

9 The great Salvation thou hast wrought,
    I'll to the World proclaim;
    The scattered Nations shall assist
    My Songs, to spread thy fame.
10 Thy Mercy reaches to the Heav'ns,
    Thy Truth unto the Skies;
11 Then let thy Glories, Lord, above
    Both Earth and Heaven rise.

Psalm LXII.

(As the 25 Psalm.)

1 MY Soul doth wait on God,
    My Rock and my defence;
2 I shall not greatly then be mov'd,
    For safety comes from thence.
3 Ye people trust in him
    What time you are afraid;

                           He'll

He'll be your refuge in diſtreſs,
    When you implore his aid.

9 The men of low degree
    Are vain; great men a lie;
Both, in the balance laid, appear
    Lighter than vanity.
10 Wealth makes not happy men,
    And truſt in this is vain,
Then ſeek not by oppreſſive arts,
    Or fraud t'increaſe your gain.

If riches ſhould abound
    By heavens bleſſing ſent;
Take heed they do not gain your hearts,
    Or make you inſolent.
11 That all may know from whence
    Their help they ſhould derive;
Thou, Lord, haſt oft declar'd, that pow'r
    Is thy Prerogative.

12 And that unceſſant ſtreams
    Of mercy flow from thee;
So that according to mens works
    Their due reward ſhall be.

Pſalm LXIII.

1 EArly, O Lord, my fainting Soul
    Thy Mercy do's implore;
No Travellour in deſart Lands
    Can thirſt for Water more.
2 I long t'appear as I was wont,
    Within thy holy place,

                                     Thy

Thy Pow'r and Glory to behold,
    And to obtain thy Grace.

3 For Life it self, without thy Love,
    No relifh do's afford;
No other joys can equal this,
    To ferve and praife the Lord.
4 I'll therefore make my Pray'rs to thee,
    And blefs thee whilft I live;
5 This, like the choiceft dainties, will
    Both food and pleafure give,

6 When others fleep, my wakefull thoughts
    Prefent thee to my mind;
And in the night I think how good
    My God has been, and kind,
7 Since thou alone haft been my help,
    To thee alone I fly;
And on thy watchfull providence
    With chearfulnefs rely.

8 Dangers, whilft thou art near to me,
    Do threaten me in vain;
When I keep clofe to God, his care
    And Pow'r will me fuftain.

Pfalm LXV.

(*As the* 100 *Pfalm.*)

1 PRaifes in Sion wait for thee,
    And there the Vow perform'd fhall be.

2 To thee, O God, that heareſt Pray'r,
All fleſh ſhall chearfully repair.

3 Our Sins may juſtly put a ſtop,
To all that good from thee we hope;
Thy Mercy do's thoſe fears allay,
For this will purge our ſins away.

4 O happy they that may draw near
To thee, and in thy Courts appear;
For theſe ſhall all refreſhments have,
Thy Houſe can give, or they can crave.

5 By thy amazing wonders, thou
Thy kindneſs to the good doſt ſhow;
The ends of th' Earth in thee confide,
And th' Iſles that in the Sea reſide.

6 Mountains that ſeem to touch the Skie,
Gain from thy ſtrength ſtability;
7 The roaring Seas God do's aſſwage,
And ſtills the peoples madder rage.

Part, II.

8 O'er all the Earth the Nations ſpread,
Thy works of pow'r and anger dread;
And all adore thy goodneſs great,
Where e'er the Sun do's riſe or ſet.

9 Thy care prevents a threatning Dearth;
Thou viſiteſt the thirſty Earth;
Showres to inrich her barren Womb
From thy full Springs above do come.

Thy Bounty do's that food provide,
By which our needs are all ſupply'd.

E

10

10 The hardned ridges of the Field,
   Water'd with showres, are soft and yield.

   Its Furrows setled and deprest,
   Its Spring by after Rains is blest.
11 The fruitfull year thy blessings Crown,
   And plenty from the Clouds drop down

12 The Wilderness refresht with rain,
   Tho' parch'd before, now Springs again:
   The little Hills new Garments wear,
   And in their youthfull green appear.

13 Flocks are the Cloathing of the Plain,
   The Vales are cover'd o'er with grain.
   All nature seems to shout and sing,
   To welcome in the hopefull Spring,

Psalm LXVI.

1 LEt all the Earth with joy resound,
     To God their voices raise;
2 Extoll him in their Songs, and make
     Him glorious by their praise.
3 Proclaim his mighty works, in which
     Such terrour do's appear;
   As makes his Foes to crouch, and feign
     Obedience through their fear.

4 Ev'n all the Earth shall Worship thee,
     And sing unto thy name:
5 To see the wonders thou hast wrought,
     To raise and spread thy Fame.

6 He

6 He turn'd the Sea into dry Land;
  The swelling Flood made way
For Israel to pass; who there
  His glories did display.

7 He views the Nations, and his Rule
  Do's o'er the world extend;
Then let not men rebell; for pride
  Will in their ruine end.

8 Let all the people bless the Lord,
  And loudly sing thy praise;
9 Thou great Preserver of our Lives,
  And Guide of all our ways.

Part, II.

13 I'll go into thine House, O Lord,
  And thankfull offerings lay
14 Before thy Altar; and the vows
  I made in trouble, pay.

15 To honour, him from whom all good
  Do's come, I'll spare no cost;
I'll offer what he do's require,
  And what will please him most,

16 You that are pious, come and hear
  What God for me has done;
His mercies show'd to me, will be
  For your instruction.

17 When I with grief opprest to him
  My fervent cryes did raise;
He heard me gratiously, and turn'd
  My sighing into praise.

E 2

18 God will not favour me, if I
     Iniquity regard:
19 But he inclin'd his Ear to me
     And my Petitions heard.
20 O let the glorious Name of God
     Be ever magnify'd;
Who neither did reject my Pray'r,
     Nor his own Grace deny'd.

Psalm LXVII.

1 SHew mercy to us, Lord,
     Bless us with gifts divine;
O let the Glories of thy face,
     On us thy Servants shine.
2   May thy hid ways be known,
     Thy fear on Earth abound;
And thy Salvation over all
     The Heathen World resound.

3   Let all in Psalms of praise
     Their gratefull thoughts express;
Let all the people round the World
     Thy mighty Name confess.
4   The Nations now may sing
     Their joys, since God do's reign:
He rules with wisedom, this great Judge
     Will righteousness maintain.
5   Let all in Psalms of praise
     Their gratefull thoughts express;
Let all the people round the World
     Thy mighty Name confess.

6 Then

5 Then shall th' enriched Earth
  With Plenty overflow;
And God on all his other gifts,
  His blessing will bestow.

7 His blessings showr'd on us,
  Our happy days shall crown;
His pow'r and greatness all the World
  With humble fear shall own.

Psalm LXVIII.

(As the 100 *Psalm.*)

1 LEt the Great God arise, and then
  His scattered Foes will flee for fear;
2 Vanish like Smoak, and melt like Wax
Before the Fire, when he draws near.

3 But let the Just rejoyce. and praise
4 His name, to whom all pow'r belongs;
He rides on High above the Clouds,
Let him be rais'd too in your Songs;

5 He pities Orphans, widdows wrongs
6 He rights, brings chained Prisoners out;
He for the desolate provides,
But plagues the Rebels land with drought.

7 Lord, when thou brought'st thy people forth
From Egypt, with a mighty hand;
And led'st them through the Wilderness,
To bring them to the promis'd land.
8 The Heav'ns before thy Lightnings dropt,
The Earth did with thy Thunder quake;

E 3   Mount

Mount Sinai, when the Lord came down,
Did from its firm foundation shake.

17 Thousands of Angels (Heav'ns great Host)
Like Guards took up their Station there;
God's special presence was declar'd,
When these Attendants did appear.

Part. II.

18 Our God, like a great Conquerour,
Ascended is above the Skies;
And after him in triumph draws,
As spoils, his Captiv'd Enemies.

He scattered his various gifts
Around, to make his Bounty known;
Ev'n Rebels had a share, 'mongst whom
He dwells, and they his kindness own.

19 God heaps his daily benefits
On us, and he shall have our Songs;
20 He is our Saviour, to whom
The Pow'r of Life and Death belongs.

21 In his just vengeance he shal wound
The heads of all that him resist;
On whom no methods of his Love
Prevail, but still in sin persist.

22 Praise him, ye Kingdoms of the Earth!
33 Who governs all the Heav'nly Spheres;
From thence he Thunders with his voice,
Which every Creature dreads that hears

34 Give him the Glory of his Pow'r,
Illustriously to Israel shown;

Its

Its wonders in the Heav'ns appear,
And thence by all the World is known.

35 They that behold his Majesty
In holy places, are amaz'd;
'Tis God that Giveth strength and pow'r
Unto his Saints. His Name be prais'd,

Psalm LXX.

(As the 25 Psalm.)

1 BEhold my Troubles, Lord,
How they with haste advance;
O do not stay, but come as fast
To my deliverance:

2 Let those that seek my life,
Their own confusion meet;
When they attempt my hurt, with shame,
Be forced to retreat.

3 Let such as make my griefs
Their sport, unpitied be;
Those that deride my trust in God,
Reward with infamy.

4 But all true worshippers
That seek their God to please,
Thy favour towards them express,
And make their joys t'increase.

Let those that hope in thee,
And thy Salvation love,
Ever have cause, and hearts to say,
Praised be God above,

5   Look on my state opprest
    With misery and grief;
Thou art my Saviour and my help;
    Lord, send me quick relief.

Psalm LXXI.

(*As the 25 Psalm.*)

1 MY Soul on God relies,
    Let none disgrace my trust;
2 Lord, hear and save me when I call,
    As thou art good and just.
3   Be thou my sure defence,
    Whereto I may resort;
Make good thy gratious promise. Lord,
    Be thou my Rock and Fort.

4   Save me from cruel men,
    And those that are unjust;
Thou, Lord, alone hast been my hope,
    And from my youth, my Trust.
6   Thou took'st me from the Womb,
    When my first breath I drew;
Thou hast sustain'd me ever since,
    All praise to thee is due.

7   Many with wonder gaze
    On me, as one forlorn;
8 But by my praises and thine aid,
    I shall confute their scorn.
9   Lord, when my strength decays,
    And when my years decline,

Do not forsake or cast me of,
But own me still for thine.

14 In thee I'll place my hopes,
Thee with more praises crown;

15 Thy Truth and Mercies I'll proclaim,
Whose measures are unknown.

Part. II.

16 To no supports I'll fly,
But to the strength divine;
No other goodness shall be nam'd,
Or faithfulness, but thine.

17 These from my youth I've learnt;
And hitherto declar'd
Thy wonderous works. Forsake me not

18 Now when I am grey-hair'd.

Till I have farther shown
Thy pow'r, and taught thy fear,
Both to the present age, and those
That after shall appear.

19 Thy goodness, Lord, is great,
Thy works illustrious are;
All thy perfections have no bounds,
None can with thee compare.

20 Thou shalt again revive
My Soul, with grief deprest;

21 Thou, Lord, wilt raise my low estate,
Comfort and give me rest.

22 Then to proclaim thy Truth,
I'll all my Powers raise;

E 5   And

And to improve my Songs, will add
Sweet instruments of praise.

23 My chearfull tongue and lips,
Shall loudly bear a part
In praising thee, when tun'd and rais'd
By a most thankfull heart.
24 This shall be my great work,
To celebrate thy fame;
Who hast redeemed me, and brought
Mine Enemies to shame.

Psalm LXXIII.

(As the 100 Psalm.)

1 CErtain it is, that God is kind
To those that are sincerely good;
2 But yet my Faith was at a loss,
My feet did stagger where I stood.

3 I saw the wickeds prosperous state,
My envy at those Fools did rise;
4 That, when a healthfull Age was past,
A quiet Death should close their Eyes.

5 Exempt from Plagues and miseries
That others seek t'escape in vain;
6 They're covered o'er with violence,
And Pride surrounds them like a Chain.

7 Pamper'd with ease and luxury,
Their Body thrives, looks fat and fair;

Their

Their wealth rolls in with a full tide,
Beyond their hopes, without their care.

8 Such is their Pride, that they profeſs
Oppreſſive courſes without ſhame;
9 Dare Heav'n it ſelf with blaſphemies,
And freely blaſt the good man's name.

10 This gives diſturbance to his mind,
And paſſion makes his tears to flow;
11 Doubts riſe within him, whether God
Diſcerns or minds things done below.

12 Th' ungodly are the proſperous men,
Thrive in the World and riches gain;
13 I've waſh'd my hands in innocence,
And cleans'd my heart, ſays he, in vain.

14 For every morn renews my Plagues,
And I whole days in ſorrow ſpend.
15 But ſtay; thus ſpeaking, I againſt
The Faith of all good men offend.

Part. II.

16 I oft conſider'd with my ſelf
Th' unequal ways of Providence;
I found them hard to be reſolv'd,
And doubts long kept me in ſuſpence.

17 At laſt I enquired at God's Houſe,
And there did my miſtakes amend;
Before I onely view'd their way,
But now I underſtood their end.

18 I ſaw the ſlippery precipice
On which their tottering feet were plac'd;

19 And with what Terrours they were seis'd
    When down to sudden ruine cast.

20 Their happiness was like a Dream,
    Or shade that quickly vanishes;

21 Lord! what a stupid beast was I,

22 To vex my self at their success.

23 For all this while I was thy care,
    By thee sustain'd, tho' suffering;

24 Thy Counsels here shall guide me still,
    And afterward to Glory bring.

25 Lord, there is none in Heav'n or Earth,
    On whom I can rely, like thee;

26 For when my heart and hopes here fail,
    My stay and Portion thou wilt be.

27 But those that are from God estrang'd,
    Or unto hatefull Idols bow,
    Shall surely their own ruine meet,
    And a deserved overthrow,

28 God is my chiefest Good: 'tis best
    To keep me to my God most nigh;
    Then I his Mercy and his Truth
    Shall praise, when I on him rely.

Psalm LXXXII.

(As the 113 *Psalm.)*

1 YE Rulers of the World, that bear
    God's Name, and represent him here,
    Know that this Judge among you sits.

2 If you enact unrighteous Laws,

Or

Or countenance a wicked cause,
Your guiltiness no Plea admits

5 You act like God, when you defend
The poor, and your assistance lend
To helpless men that Justice crave.
6 Absolve the Innocent with speed,
Obnoxious onely by their need,
And from th' Oppressours Power save.

5 They cry too oft to you in vain,
Who'll know no other right but gain,
Whose Eyes are blind by Bribes you take.
Thus Justice cannot find its course,
But Laws neglected lose their force,
And all the Lands Foundations shake.

6 I said y'are Gods, but you shall die,
And fall, tho' Sons of the Most High,
7 As other Men and Kings have done.
2 Arise, great Judge of all, and reign,
Fall'n Justice then will rise again,
When God doth sit upon his Throne.

Psalm LXXXIV.

1 HOw beauteous is the place where thou
Thy presence, Lord, dost grant!
2 Oh how I long t'approach thy Courts,
Impatient of restraint!
3 The little Birds the Liberties
Enjoy, which I'm deny'd;
Near to thine Altars they prepare
Their Nests, and there reside.

4 Oh happy men! that may frequent
    Thine House, to praise thee still;
5 Whose trust is in thine aid, whose heart
    Devout affections fill.
8 Great God of Hosts, attend when I
    My Pray'r to thee address;
9 Look gratiously on mine Estate,
    And thine Anointed bless.
10 A thousand joyous days elsewhere,
    Yield me not such content,
    As one days freedom at thy House,
    And in thy service spent.
    There let me have the meanest place,
    And at the threshold lye;
    Rather than all the wickeds State
    Without this liberty.
11 God is a glorious Sun, from whom
    We Light and Life derive;
    A Shield for our defence, and he
    Will Grace and Glory give.
    No good will he with-hold, from him
    That's upright in his way.
12 Oh happy man! that makes the Lord
    His onely trust and stay.

Psalm LXXXV.

(As the 113 Psalm.)

1 THy Mercy, Lord, has chang'd our doom,
    Thy Captives to their Land are come,
                                    And

And all their sins are done away.

3 Thine Anger which was fierce before,
Is now remov'd and flames no more;
O let it ever cease, we pray.

5 When wilt thou, Lord, from wrath refrain?
6 Raise and revive our joys again?
7 Thy saving mercies, Lord, restore.
8 I'll listen to the voice of Peace,
Which God will to his Saints express,
If they return to sin no more.

9 Surely thy saving help is near
To such as thee sincerely fear,
And glory to our Land will bring.
10 Mercy and Truth together meet,
Justice and Peace each other greet,
11 And truth out of the Earth shall spring.

From Heav'n shall righteousness look
down;
12 God with his Blessings will us Crown,
Our Land with Plenty shall o'erflow.
When Righteousness prepares his way,
Justice with us shall longer stay,
And Mercy tread where this do's go.

Psalm LXXXVI.

1 LOrd, bow thine Ear to my requests,
Tho' poor and in the dust;
2 O save my righteous Soul, for, Lord,
In thee alone I trust.

3 Be mercifull to me, O God,
    And hear my mournfull voice;
4 Daily my Soul to thee ascends,
    Oh make it to rejoice.

5 Thou, Lord, art gratious and good,
    To pardon sins inclin'd;
And all that humbly thee implore,
    Shall plenteous mercy find.
6 To thee I call in my distress,
    In hope thou wilt attend;
7 On thee with patience wait, till thou
    A gratious answer send.

8 Tho' Heathens boast of other Gods,
    And talk of Pow'rs Divine:
There's none that can compare with thee,
    Nor any works like thine.
9 All the deceived Lands at length
    Their Maker shall adore;
Shall glorify thy Name, O Lord,
    And celebrate thy Pow'r.

10 When they behold how great thou art,
    What wonders thou hast done;
Their Idols they'll disown; and say,
    That thou art God alone.

Part. II.

11 Lord, guide my steps, that from the way
    Of truth I ne'er may err;
My loose affections so unite,
    That I thy name may fear.

12 With

12 With all my Soul I'll praise the Lord,
    His glories ever tell;
13 By whose great goodness I have been
    Freed from the lowest Hell.

15 Thou, Lord, art pitifull and kind,
    To punish Sinners slow;
Goodness and faithfulness from thee
Abundantly do flow.
16 Thy mercifull regard I need,
    And strength from thee I crave;
From all designed mischiefs, Lord,
Thy humble servant save.

17 Some signal mark of favour show,
    Which all my Foes may see,
And at their malice blush; when thou
Dost help and comfort me.

Psalm LXXXIX.

1 THY Mercies, Lord, I'll ever sing,
    Thy truth to all proclaim;
5 The Heav'nly Angels sacred Quire
Shall celebrate the same.
6 These never with the Lord compare,
    Nor his Commands contest;
7 But give attendance at his Throne,
    With awfull fear possess'd.

8 Great God! there's none that's arm'd with
    Or girt with Truth like thee;   (pow'r,

F   2Thou,

9 Thou, when the Waves arise, dost rule
    And still the raging Sea.
10 Thy arm alone brake Egypts pow'r;
    And Israel did adore,
When they beheld the drowned Host
    Lie scattered on the shore.
11 The World with all therein, is thine,
    Made by thy pow'rfull voice;
12 With all the Quarters of the Earth,
    Which in thy care rejoice.
13 Thy great and uncontrolled Pow'r
    Can no resistance fear;
14 Yet Mercy, Righteousness and Truth,
    In all thy Rule appear.
15 Blest are the Men that understand
    The joyfull sound of praise;
They through thy favour shall enjoy
    Pleasant and happy days.
16 Th' expressions of thy wond'rous Love
    Will fresh delights creare;
And thou, the Glory of their strength,
    Wilt raise their low Estate.

Psalm XC.

(As the 100 *Psalm.)*

1 LOrd, every Age and Race has seen,
    Thou hast our help and refuge been.
2 E're that the Mountains had a Birth,
    Or ever thou hadst form'd the Earth.

Thou

Thou hadſt a being long before,
And ſhalt abide when time's no more.

3 Thy firſt Decree'gainſt man was juſt,
Bidding him Turn again to Duſt.

4 A thouſand years, if we could ſtay
In Life ſo long, is but a day.
Compar'd with thee; and in thy ſight,
Like the ſhort Watches of the Night.

5 Death like an over-flowing ſtream
Sweeps us away; our Life's a Dream.

6 Like Flow'rs ith' Morning freſh and fair,
Cut down e're Night, and withered are.

7 Thine Anger and our Wickedneſs,

8 Makes the ſhort Term of Nature leſs;

9 And thus our years to'an end are brought,
As ſwiftly as a breath or thought.

10 Our Age to Seventy years is ſet;
If to another Stage we get,
And unto Fourſcore years arrive,
We rather ſigh and groan, than live.

Part. II.

11 Lord, who enough conſidered hath
The Pow'r and Terrour of thy wrath?
Wrath that is equal to our dread,
And ſtrikes ſo often Sinners dead.

12 Oh that the ſenſe of our laſt end,
And Sorrows that this Life attend,
May more excite our fear of thee,
And a wiſe care of Piety.

13 When,

13   When, Lord, shall thy displeasure cease?
    When wilt thou give our troubles ease?
    Now we are humble and repent,
    Shew pity to us and relent.

14   Oh let that mercy come at last,
    We long impatiently to tast:
15   And in proportion to our tears,
    Let Gladness crown our future years.

16   Since Acts of grace thy Glory are,
    And please thee most; do thou appear
    In those to us and to our Race:
17   Shew us the Beauties of thy Face.

    Afford thy Light to guide our way,
    That we may never go astray:
    All our good undertakings bless,
    And prosper with desir'd success.

Psalm XCI.

(*As the* 100 *Psalm.*)

2   HE that has God for his retreat,
     Has gain'd a safe and quiet seat.
    For God's o'er-spreading Providence
    Will like a shade be his Defence.

2   To him as to my Fort I'll fly;
    On him, my pow'rfull God, rely.
3   When noysome Plagues infect the air,
    He'll save thee from the secret snare.

4   His care, like Wings, shall safety yield,
    His faithfull promise be thy shield:

5 So that no dangers of the Night
Shall seise thee with a sudden fright.

6 Plagues that like poisoned Arrows kill,
And all arround with slaughter fill,
Walking unseen both Night and Day,
Shall miss their aim, or balk their way.

7 Thousands shall fall on every hand,
And thou the while unhurt shalt stand:

8 And onely with thine Eyes shalt see
What shall the wickeds portion be.

Part. II.

9 Since thou hast made the Lord most High
Thy Refuge and Security;

10 No evil shall thy joys molest,
Nor Plague thy dwelling shall infest.

11 Blest Angels charg'd to guard thy way,
To thee shall kind attendance pay.

12 These in their hands shall thee support,
Lest thou shouldst stumble to thy hurt.

13 The Lyon thou maist safely meet,
Tread th' Aspe and Dragon under feet.

14 Since he has set his Love on me,
From danger I will set him free.

Because he knows and fears my Name,
I'll honour him and raise his Fame.

15 When he invokes me in his need,
I'll hear and answer him with speed.

When he's in Trouble I'll stand by,
To save, and set him up on High.

19 Give him long Life; and when that's done,
    Will shew him my Salvation.

Psalm XCII.

1 O What a pleasant work it is,
      To praise the Lord above;
2 Morning and Evening to proclaim
      His faithfulness and Love;
2 Sweet Notes of Instruments to joyn
      With an Harmonious voice!
4 Thy gratious dealings with me, Lord,
      Have made me to rejoice.

5 Great are thy works, and thy designs
      Contain the deepest sense;
6 Tho' wicked Men and Fools mistake
      Thy ways of Providence,
7 They spring and flourish like the Grass,
      With good success o'er joy'd:
   And onely grow to be mown down,
      And utterly destroy'd.

12 But righteous men like fruitfull Palms,
      Or stately Cedars grow:
   For planted in thy Courts, they're fed
      With Springs that ever flow.
14 There they are fair and ever thrive,
      And still more fruit shall bring:
   Age that makes other things decay,
      Makes them more flourishing.

15 Thus God appears to all the World
      To be both good and just;

No

No falseness can be charg'd on him
That is my Rock and trust.

Psalm XCIII.

(As the 100 *Psalm.*)

1 THe Lord do's reign, and like a King
      Puts on his Robes of Glorious Light ;
Tremble thou Earth, when he appears
Cloathed and girt about with might.

Under his Rule th'unquiet World
Will gain stability and peace ;
2 Of old his Empire did begin,
And, like himself, can never cease.

3 In vain the Worlds rebellious pow'rs
In Tumults and Commotions rise ;
Like troubled Waters of the Sea,
That bid Defiance to the Skies.

4 Resist not his unequal strength,
That's far above your threatning noise ;
For ev'n the Seas unruly Waves
Do calmly listen to his voice.

5 Lord, as thy Pow'r can never fail,
So all thy promises are sure :
'Tis thy Perfection to be true,
And theirs that serve thee, to be pure.

Psalm

Psalm XCIII.

(Another Metre.)

1 THE Lord do's reign, and cloaths himself
　With Robes of glorious Light:
Tremble thou Earth, when he appears
　Girded about with might.
Now the unquiet World will gain
　Stability and peace,
2 His Empire was of old, and like
　Himself can never cease.

3 In vain the Worlds rebellious pow'rs
　Combin'd in Tumults rise;
Like Waters of the Sea, that bid
　Defiance to the Skies.
4 Resist not his unequal strength,
　That's far above your noise;
For ev'n the Seas unruly Waves
　Are calmed at his voice.

5 Thy power, Lord, can never fail,
　Thy Promises are sure;
Thy Glory's to be true, and theirs
　That serve thee, to be pure.

Psalm XCIV.

1 THou great Avenger of all wrong,
　At length thy Justice shew;

2 Ari-

2 Arife, and render to the Proud
   Rewards that are their due.
3 How long fhall evil men triumph,
   And boaft their Villanies;
4 Speak fcornfully of God himfelf,
   And Providence defpife?

5 Who, whilft the ruine of the poor
6   And innocent they plot,
7 Say that the Lord do's not difcern,
   Or elfe regards it not.
8 When will thefe brutifh Sinners learn,
   Thefe fenfelefs Fools be wife?
9 Shall not he hear that made the Ears,
   And fee that form'd the Eyes?

10 He the rude Nations do's inftruct,
   And teaches Man his skill:
   Shall not he know then, and chaftife
   Thy difobedient will?
11 O flatter not thy felf, nor thefe.
   Impieties maintain:
   God knows thefe very thoughts of thine,
   How falfe they are and vain.

Part. II.

12 Lord, he's a happy man, whom thou
   By chaftifements haft taught;
   And thereby to a fenfe of thee,
   And of his Duty brought.
13 God in his Mercy will at length
   From troubles fet him free;
Whilft

Whilst vengeance ruins wicked men
    Short-liv'd prosperity.

14 Tho' good men for a while chastis'd
    May under troubles grone;
God will not utterly forsake,
    Nor cast away his own.
15 Neglected judgment shall return
    Again to act its part;
And then felicity shall crown
    The men of upright heart.

16 T'oppose my wicked Foes, I call'd
    To other aids in vain;
17 Without thy succours, in the Grave
    I and my hopes had lain.
18 When I despair'd to keep my feet,
    Thy mercy me upheld:
Thy comforts eas'd my troubled thoughts,
    And swelling passions quell'd.

Psalm XCV.

(*As the* 100 *Psalm.*)

1 COme let us all unite our joys,
    And to the Lord our voices raise;
2 Before his presence let us come
    With thankfull hearts and Psalms of praise.

3 Our Lord is a great God and King,
    Of power super-Eminent

                Abo-

Above all Gods; him Angels serve,
And Princes onely represent.

4 The secret places of the Earth,
  And strength of Hills are in his hand:
5 He made the Waters of the Sea,
  And for their bound prepar'd the Land.

6 To him that made us let us kneel,
  And humble Adorations give ;
7 Who are the people of his care,
  The Sheep that on his pastures live.

8 To day let's hearken to his voice,
  And not such hardned Sinners prove,
9 As those that in the Wilderness
  Provok'd and tempted God above.

They prov'd his pow'r, and saw his works,
10 And griev'd his Patience fourty year ;
  Till, wearied with their murmurings,
  That Race he could no longer bear.

He did their stupid unbelief,
  And base Ingratitude detest ;
11 And in his Indignation sware
  They should not come into his Rest.

Psalm XCV.

(Another Metre.)

1 COme let us with united joys
  To God our voices raise:

2 With thankfull hearts before him come,
  And loudly sing his praise.

3 Our Lord is a great God and King,
  In power eminent
Above all Gods: him Angels serve,
  And Princes represent.

4 The secrets of the Earth, and strength
  Of Hills are in his hand;
5 He made the Waters of the Sea,
  And for their bound, dry land.

6 To him that made us, let us kneel,
  And Adorations give;
7 Who are his people, and the Sheep
  That on his pastures live.

8 To day let's hear his voice, and not
  Such hardned Sinners prove,
9 As those that in the Wilderness
  Provoked God above.

They prov'd his pow'r, and saw his works,
10 And griev'd him fourty year;
  Till, wearied with that murm'ring Race,
He could no longer bear,

He did their unbelief, and base
  Ingratitude detest;
11 And in his Anger sware, they should
  Not come into his Rest.

Psalm XCVI.

(*As the* 100 *Psalm.*)

1 LEt all the Earth their voices raise,
  To sing the choicest Psalm of praise;

2 To

2 To sing and bless God's sacred name,
And all his saving works proclaim.

3 His Glory let the Heathen know,
His wonders to the Nations show;

4 Let him be prais'd that is so high;
More fear'd than any Deity:

5 For Heathen Gods but Creatures are;
He made the Heav'ns and every Star.

6 He in Majestick splendor dwells
In Beauty and in strength excells.

7 Let every Tongue and every Tribe,
Glory and Pow'r to God ascribe:

8 The Glory give that is his due,
Their Off'rings in his Courts renew.

9 Fall down before him, and confess
His Majesty and Holiness;
Let all the Earth the Lord revere,
And by their Duty shew their fear.

10 Say to the World th' Almighty reigns;
A Judge that equity maintains;
He'll make their Wars and Tumults cease,
And bless the Earth with quiet peace.

11 Let Heav'n and Earth then tell their joys,
The Ocean by its roaring noise;

12 Fields by the fairness of their Crops,
Trees by the Fruits that Crown their Tops,

13 At his approach all Nature's glad,
And onely Sinners are afraid:
All whom he judges shall confess
His equity and Righteousness.

Psalm

Pſalm XCVII.

(As the 100 *Pſalm.)*

1 LEt th' Earth rejoice, ſince God do's reign:
  For tho' thick darkneſs do's ſurround,
  And cloud his ways of Providence,
  Yet perfect juſtice is their ground,

3 When God prepares himſelf for wrath,
4 His Lightnings flame around the Skies;
  A dreadfull Fire before him goes,
  To burn up all his Enemies.

  Th' amazed Earth ſees this and quakes,
5 The Hills like melted Wax flow down;
6 The Heav'ns his Juſtice do proclaim,
  And Men below his Glories own.

7 Confounded be thoſe Worſhippers,
  That to a graven Image bow,
  And boaſt of Idols; worſhip him,
  Angels above and Gods below.

8 Good men will hear the news with Joy,
  When Judgments on theſe Sinners fall;
9 Which tell the World their Gods are vain,
  And thou art high above them all.

10 All ye that Love and ſerve the Lord,
  Strictly preſerve your innocence;
  Then let the wicked ſeek your fall,
  God will ſtand up for your defence.

11

11 Th' immortal Seeds of light and bliss,
For truely pious men are sown :
A joyfull Harvest will at length
Their labours and their sorrows Crown.

12 Then let your chearfull temper show,
The God you serve is good and kind:
Praise him for all his Mercies past,
And wait with joy for those behind.

Psalm XCVII.

(*Another Metre*)

1 GOD Reigns, let all the Earth rejoyce:
Tho' darkness may surround
And Cloud his ways of providence,
Yet Justice is their ground.
3 Lightnings, when God prepares for wrath,
Do flame around the Skies;
4 A Fire before him goes, to burn
Up all his Enemies.

The Earth sees this and quakes, the Hills
5 Like melted Wax flow down;
6 The Heav'ns his Righteousness declare,
And Men his Glories own.
7 Confounded be those Worshippers,
That to an Image bow,
And boast of Idols; worship him,
Angels and Gods below.

8 Good

8 Good men will joy, when punishments
    Shall on these Sinners fall;
9 Which shew their Gods are vain, and thou
    Art high above them all.
10 All ye that love and fear the Lord,
    Preserve your innocence;
Then let the wicked seek your fall,
    God will be your defence.

11 Th'immortal Seeds of light and bliss
    For pious men are sown;
A joyfull Harvest will at length
    Their work and sorrows crown.
12 Then let your chearfull temper show
    The God you serve is kind;
Praise him for Mercies past, and wait
    With joy for those behind.

Psalm XCVIII.

1 REnew your Songs to God, and tell
    What wonders he hath done;
Let all proclaim the Victories
    His pow'rfull Arm has won.
2 His Mercy which was kept before
    A secret and inclos'd;
Now to the clear and open view
    Of Heathens is expos'd.

3 His promis'd goodness and his Truth
    Was first to Israel shown;
But now the ends of th'Earth have seen
    His great Salvation.

8 Good men will joy, when punishments
  Shall on these Sinners fall;
6 Joyn Musick to their Hymns of praise,
  To testifie their joys.

7 Let swelling Seas roar, and excite
  The joys of Neighbouring lands;
8 Let Echoing Hills the noise repeat,
  And Rivers clap their hands.
9 Whole Nature well may feel a change
  When God's approach is nigh:
  Who comes to judge and rule the World
  With Truth and Equity.

Psalm C.

1 LEt all the Nations of the Earth,
  To God their chearfull voices raise;
2 With Gladness worship him, and come
  Before his Face with Songs of praise.

3 Know that our Lord is God alone
  Who did to all their beings give;
  We are the people of his Care,
  The Sheep that on his pastures live.

4 Enter his Gates with thankfull hearts,
  His praises in his Courts proclaim;
  And let his pow'rfull love excite
  Each Soul to bless his Sacred Name.

5 For God is infinitely good,
  His mercy is for ever sure;

G   His

His Truth from Generation
To Generation shall endure.

Psalm CII.

1 LOrd hear the Pray'rs and mournfull cries
　　Of mine afflicted State;
2 And with thy Comforts chear my Soul,
　　Before it be too late.
11 My days, like the declining shades,
　　Make haste and fly away;
　　As Flow'rs before the scortching Sun,
　　They wither and decay.

24 Lord take me not away before
　　My better days be past;
　　Thine undeclining years beyond
　　All Generations last.
25 Th' unknown Foundations of the Earth
　　Of old by thee were laid;
　　The Fair and Beauteous Heavens shew
　　The work thy hands have made.

26 These all shall perish, and wax old
　　Like Garments thrown aside;
　　But when they change, thy years ne'er fail,
27　　Thou dost the same abide.
28 Thy Kindness to the good is firm,
　　Thy word to them is sure;
　　Tho' strange Events may change the World,
　　Their Race shall still endure.

Psalm

Psalm CIII.

(*As the* 100 *Psalm.*)

1 BLess thou the Lord, my Soul; his name
    Let all the pow'rs within me bless;
2 O let not his past favours lie
Forgotten in unthankfulness.

3 It's he that pardons all thy sins,
He that in sickness makes thee sound:
4 It's he redeemed from the Grave
Thy Life, with Love and Mercy Crown'd.

5 It's he that fills thy mouth with good,
And all thy just desires supplies:
Who, like the Eagles, makes thine Age
    To a renewed youth arise.

6 From his strict justice sure relief
Oppressed Innocence shall find:
7 Moses and Israel knew his ways,
And th'inclinations of his mind,

8 Abundant Mercies flow from God,
Love is his Nature and Delight;
9 Slow is his Wrath, and tho' he chides,
Intends not to destroy us quite.

His Anger in its rise and stay,
From Rules of Justice never swerves;
10 And when he punishes our faults,
The measure's less than sin deserves;

11 As Heav'n is far above the Earth,
So his Rewards exceed our Love;
      G 2   12 Far-

12 Farther than Eaſt is from the Weſt,
    His pardon do's our ſins remove.

Part. II.

13 A Father's pity to his Child,
    Reſembles God's, tho' ſhorter far;
14 For he conſiders our weak Frame,
    That onely quickned Duſt we are.

15 Man's days are like the Graſs, or Flow'r
    That in the Field its beauty ſhows;
16 But fades with every blaſting wind,
    And then its former place none knows.

17 But God's Eternal Truth and Love,
    Is to good men and to their race:
18 Thoſe that his Laws and Covenant keep,
    His favour ever will embrace.

19 Circled with glorious Light, his Throne
    The Lord has plac'd in Heav'n above;
    Whoſe mighty Pow'r and Sovereign Rule,
    Extends o'er all that Live and Move.

20 Bleſs God ye Angels, who in ſtrength
    And ready ſervices tranſcend;
21 Bleſs him ye Hoſts and Miniſters,
    Who all, to do his will, attend.

22 All ye his works, that ſubject are
    In every place to his controll;
    Bleſs ye your Maker; and with them
    Joyn in his praiſes, O my Soul.

Pſalm

Psalm CIII.

(another Metre)

1 MY Soul bless thou the Lord, his Name
    All Pow'rs within me bless;
2 O never let his favours be
    Lost in unthankfulness.
3 It's he forgives thy sins, and do's
    Thy sicknesses remove;
4 It's he redeems thee from the Grave,
    And Crowns thy Life with Love.

5 It's he that fills thy mouth with good,
    Thy just desires supplies;
Who, like the Eagles, makes thine Age
    To a new youth arise.
6 From his strict justice sure relief,
    Wrong'd Innocence shall find:
7 Moses, his ways; and Israel knew
    Th' Intentions of his mind.

8 The Lord is Kind; and Goodness is
    His Nature and Delight;
9 Slow is his wrath, and tho' he chides,
    Would not destroy us quite.
His anger in its rise and stay
    From Justice never swerves:
10 And when he punishes our faults,
    It's less than sin deserves,

11 As Heav'n do's far exceed the Earth,
    So his Rewards our Love:
12 Farther than East is from the West,
    He do's our sins remove.

Part. II.

13 A Father's pity to his Child
    Than God's is lesser far;
14 For he considers our weak Frame,
    And knows that Dust we are.
15 Man's days are like the Grass, or Flow'r
    Fresh when it's newly blown,
16 But fades with every blasting wind,
    Whose place no more is known.

17 But God is true, and ever kind
    To good men and their Race:
18 Those that his Laws and Covenant keep
    His favour will embrace.
19 Circled with Light, the Lord has plac'd
    His Throne in Heav'n above:
    Whose Sovereign Empire do's extend
    O'er all that live and move.

20 Bless God ye Angels, who in strength
    And services transcend;
21 Bless him ye Hosts and Ministers,
    Who all his will attend.
22 All ye his works in every place,
    Subject to his controll,
    Bless ye your Maker; and with them
    Joyn in his praise, my Soul.

Psalm CIV.

(*As the* 100 *Psalm.*)

1 MY Soul for ever bless the Lord;
   To this his Greatness do's invite;
Honour and Majesty s his Robe
2 His beauteous vesture splendid light.

He as a Tent the Heav'ns extends,
3 Whose Rooms on liquid Waters stay;
Clouds are his Chariot, and the Winds
With their Wing'd Wheels mete out his
         way.

4 Angels as swift as air, as bright
As flames, with quick obedience move;
To publish and effect below,
His pleasure, giv'n in charge above.

5 The Earths foundations are unknown,
No Pillars rais'd its weight to bear;
And yet no pow'r can make it move,
Tho' it hangs loose in fluid air.

6 The Earths first covering was the Deep,
Whose Waves the Highest Hills surpass'd;
7 Till at thy check and thunders voice,
They shrank and fled away in hast.

8 The Mountains by hid ways they climb,
Thence to the lower Vales descend;
Till in the Sea, whence first they came
At last their winding courses end.

9 In

9 In vain the Oceans swelling Pride,
  Threatens again the Earth to cover;
  It's fixed bounds no rising Tides,
  Without new leave, can e'er pass over.

Part. II.

10 He from the Hills, through secret veins,
  Causes the Crystal Springs to burst;
11 They glide through Vallies, where the
          Beasts,
  And the wild Asses quench their thirst.

12 There Birds are taught with curious Art
  Their Nests in shady Boughs to raise;
  And by their chearfull Notes reprove
  Our Silence in our Maker's praise.

13 Nor can the higher grounds, which gape
  For thirst, complain that they're forgot:
  Clouds big with show'rs on them distill,
  And water every barren plot.

14 By his Command th' enriched Earth
  Food for all Creatures do's produce;
  The Grass springs up to serve the Beasts,
  And Hearbs for Man's peculiar use.

15 Rich Wine that chears man's heart, and Oil
  That makes his Countenance look bright;
  Bread the support of Life; all made
  To serve our needs, or our delight.

16 Trees that on barren Hills are plac'd,
  Need not be water'd by our care;

Whe-

Where Lebanon do's highest rise,
Cedars are ever fresh and fair.

17 There Birds obtain secure retreat;
Storks for their dwelling chuse the Pine;
18 Wild Goats find refuge in the Hills,
Conies in Rocks they undermine.

Part. III.

19 The Moon whose varied Face we see,
Measures the Seasons of the Year;
And having run his daily course,
The Sun knows when to set, and where.

20 Darkness, as well as day, thou mak'st;
'Tis Night that brings wild Beasts abroad;
21 Fierce Lyons roaring for their prey,
By hunger taught, seek meat from God.

22 At the Sun's rise, those scattered Beasts
Crowd to their Dens with hasty flight;
23 Men share the Day, whose work begins
And ends together with the Light.

24 Great God! how various are thy works,
Created all with wonderous skill.
Thy Blessings, Lord, enrich the Earth,
25 And the Seas spatious bosom fill.

Whose yielding Waves the Ships divide;
There Fishes move of different size;
26 And there the great Leviathan
Do's play, and Man's attempts despise.

27 These all wait humbly to receive
Thine Alms of seasonable food:

G 5

28 And what thine opened hand bestows,
   They gather, and are fill'd with good.

Part. IV.

29 If God but in displeasure frown,
   The whole Creation needs must mourn;
   If he with-holds his breath, or theirs,
   They die, and to their dust return.

30 His quickning spirit, when it breaths,
   All things with Life and Joy endues;
   His pow'rfull word, that made the Earth
   At first, its Face again renews.

31 While this Worlds Frame and Order lasts,
   God's Glory never can be less;
   And what his wisedom made so good,
   His favour will delight to bless.

32 But let not sinfull Man presume
   God's dreadfull Anger to provoke;
   Whose Look can cause the Earth to quake,
   His Touch makes proudest Hills to smoak.

33 The Great employment of my Life
   Shall be to praise this mighty Lord;
34 To meditate his Love and Works.
   The sweetest pleasure will afford.

35 While Sinners from the Earth consume,
   No place or thought regard them more:
   Bless thou thy Maker, O my Soul,
   Let Heav'n and Earth his Name adore.

Psalm CIV.

(Another Metre.)

1 BLess thou the Lord, my Soul, to this
    His greatness do's invite;
  Honour and Majesty's his Robe,
2 His Vesture splendid Light.
3 He as a Tent the Heav'ns extends,
    Whose Rooms on Waters stay;
  Clouds are his Chariot, and the Winds
    Wing'd Wheels mete out his way.

4 Angels as swift as air, as bright
    As flames, attend and move,
  His pleasure to effect below,
    That's giv'n in charge above.
5 The Earts Foundations are unknown,
    Its weight no Pillars bear;
  Yet none can move it, tho' it hangs
    Loose in the yielding air.

6 The Earths first covering was the Deep,
    Whose Waves the Hills surpass'd:
7 Till at thy check and thunders voice,
    They shrank and fled in haste.
8 The Mountains by hid ways they climb,
    Thence to the Vales descend;
  Till in the Sea, whence first they came,
    Their winding courses end.

9 In vain the Oceans swelling pride,
    Threatens the Earth to cover;

Its

Its fixed bounds no swelling Tides
  Can, without leave, pass over,

Part, II.

10 He from the Hills by secret veins
     Makes Crystal Springs to burst;
11 The watered Valleys give all Beasts
     Drink to allay their thirst.
12 There Birds are taught their artfull Nests
     In shady boughs to raise;
    Whose chearfull notes our silence shame
     In our Creator's praise.

13 Nor can the higher grounds, which gape
     For thirst, say they're forgot;
    Clouds big with show'rs on them distill,
     And water every plot.
14 By his Command th'enriched Earth
     Do's food for all produce;
    The Grass springs up to serve the Beasts,
     And Herbs for humane use.

15 Rich Wine that chears Man's Heart, and Oil
     That makes his Face look bright;
    Bread the support of Life; all serve
     Our Needs, or our Delight.
16 The Trees on barren Hills will thrive,
     Unwatered by our care;
    Cedars i'th' heights of Lebanon,
     Are ever fresh and fair.

17 There Birds find sure retreat, the Stork
     Dwells in the lofty Pine;
                          18 Wild

18 Wild Goats in Hills, Conies are safe
    In Rocks they undermine.

Part. III.

19 The Moons oft-varied face do's shew
     The Seasons of the Year;
   After his daily course, the Sun
     Knows when to set, and where.
20 Darkness, as well as Light, thou mak'st,
     Night brings wild Beasts abroad;
21 The hungry Lyons roar for prey,
     And seek their meat from God.

22 At the Sun's rising, to their Dens
     They crowd with hasty flight;
23 Men share the day, whose work's begun,
     And finisht with the light.
24 Great God! how various are thy works,
     All made with wond'rous skill!
     Thy blessings, Lord, enrich the Earth,
25   And Seas large bosom fill.

  There go the Ships, and there do move
     Fishes of different size;
26 There great Leviathan do's play,
     And Man's attemps despise.
27 These all wait to receive thine Alms.
     Of seasonable food;
28 They gather what thine hand bestows,
     And all are fill'd with good.

                              Part.

Part. IV.

29 If God but in displeasure frown,
  All Creatures needs must mourn;
If he with-holds their breath, they die,
  And to their Dust return.
30 His quickning spirit, when it breaths,
  All things with life endues;
His pow'rfull word that made the Earth,
  Its face again renews.

31 Whilst this Worlds Frame and Order lasts,
  God's Fame will ne'er be less;
And what his Wisedom made so good,
  Will still delight to bless.

32 But let not sinfull man presume,
  God's anger to provoke;
Whose look can cause the Earth to quake,
His Touch make Hills to smoak.

33 My lifes great business shall be this,
  To praise this Mighty Lord;
34 To meditate his Love and Works,
  The sweetest Joys afford.
35 While Sinners from the Earth consume,
  No place regards them more;
Bless thou the Lord, my Soul, his name
  Let Heav'n and Earth adore.

Psalm CV.

1 O Let us all give thanks to God,
  And call upon his Name;

His

His gratious and his mighty works,
   To all the World proclaim.
2 Let us in Songs and sacred Hymns
   Our great Creator bless ;
  And what his pow'rfull hand has wrought,
   Our joyfull tongues express.

3 Give to the Lord's most holy Name,
   The praise that is his due ;
  And your unfeigned inward joys,
   By chearfull voices shew.
4 Within his Sanctuary let
   Your Pray'rs to him be made ;
  Your hopes upon his favour rest,
   And his Almighty aid.

5 O let the works that he hath done
   Your admiration move ;
  Think on the judgments of his mouth.
   And wonders of his Love.
7 We glory that this mighty Lord
   Us for his people owns ;
  Whose judgments make th' amazed Earth
   To tremble when he frowns.

8 His Covenant with his people made,
   He ever call'd to mind ;
  And will his promises fulfill
   To Ages still behind.

Psalm CVI.

1 O Render thanks unto the Lord,
   For he alone is good ;

His

His mercies they continue sure,
  As they have ever stood.
2 But equal to the Clouds height
  None can their voices raise;
Nor, as God's mighty Acts deserve,
  Can shew forth all his praise.
3 O happy they who thy just Laws
  Observe with due regard;
And by well-doing to receive
  God's mercies are prepar'd.
4 To thee I humbly look, on me
  With favour, Lord, look down;
And bless me with the saving grace
  Afforded to thine own.
5 That I the present happiness
  Of thine Elect may share;
And may hereafter sing thy praise,
  In joys that endless are.

Psalm CVII.

(*As the* 100 *Psalm.*)

1 LEt all give thanks to God above,
  So full of kindness and of Love;
Whose Mercy Ages past have known,
And those that are to come shall crown.
2 O let it be by them confess'd,
Whom he redeem'd when sore oppress'd:
3 And made the scattered people come
From all the Lands to their own home.

4 They

4 They pass'd through Desarts , where no
way
They found, nor City where to stay :
5 No food to ease their hungers rage,
Nor Water-Springs their thirst t'asswage.

6 In their distress to God they cry'd,
Who prov'd their Saviour and their guide:
7 He the right path where they should go,
And place where they should dwell, did
show.

8 Let all men praise God's goodness then,
His wonders to the Sons of Men;
9 Whose bounty longing Souls supplies,
Their craving hunger satisfies.

Part. II.

10 Those that are in dark Prisons laid,
So nigh to Death, they're in its shade;
On whom the sorrows that they bear,
Sit heavier than the Chains they wear:

11 These having proudly God withstood,
Contemn'd his Counsels for their good;
12 He then resolv'd with pain and smart,
To quell the stoutness of their heart.

Before his stroaks they could not stand,
Nor none could raise them, but his hand.
13 Then to the Lord they're forc'd to fly,
To importune his Clemency ;

Who did regard their low address,
And sav'd them out of their distress;

H　14 He

14 He chang'd their gloomy state to light,
    And brake their bands in sunder quite.

15 Let all men praise his goodness then,
    His wonders to the Sons of Men.
16 His strength, that all things do's surpass,
    Brake Bars of Ir'n, and Gates of brass.

Part. III.

17 Fools to lewd courses wholly bent,
    Prepare for their own punishment.
    Sickness and loathsome maladies,
    From Luxury and Lust arise.

18 The Glutton's appetite o'erthrown,
    His tastfull meats will not go down.
    Nature with heavy loads oppress'd,
    Beckons to Death to be releas'd.

19 Then do these frighted Sinners fly
    To God for help; whose earnest cry
    Mov'd a regard to their address,
    Heav'n sav'd them out of this distress.

20 No need of Med'cines for their cure,
    Their virtue's not so quick nor sure;
    Deaths sentence onely he repeal'd,
    He sent his word, and they were heal'd.

21 Let all men praise his goodness then,
    His wonders to the Sons of men;
22 And by their gratefull Sacrifice,
    Declare his Works and their own joys.

Part.

Part. IV

23 They whom the Ships on th'Ocean bear,
24 Do see God's works and wonders there.
25 For at his word fierce Tempests rise,
   And lift its Waves unto the Skies.

26 One while they mount to Heav'n aloft,
   They sink into the Depths as oft.
27 The Passengers strange terrours feel,
   Like Drunkards to and fro they reel.

28 Lost to all hope, to God they cry
   For help in their extremity ;
   He lends an Ear to their address,
   And brings them out of this distress,

29 For at his beck the storms asswage,
   The furious Waves depose their rage.
30 They welcome now the calm, and see
   The Haven where they wish'd to be.

31 Let all men praise God's goodness then,
   His wonders to the Sons of men ;
32 Nor onely private off'rings bring,
   But in the Church his Glories sing.

Part. V.

33 When God's provok'd, his pow'rfull hand
   Turns Rivers to a desart land ;
34 Their fruitfulness to barren grounds,
   When wickedness therein abounds.

35 Dry grounds by Springs (to shew his Love)
   To fruitfull Pastures do improve.

36 Thither the poor for dwellings flow,
   Which after to a City grow.

37 They fow the Fields and Vineyards plant,
   Whofe Fruits fupply their growing want.
38 Their Race fprings faft from fruitfull ftocks
   Their wealth increafes with their flockss

39 By Heaven bleft : but when they fin.
   They're punifht and brought low again.
40 Ev'n Princes are expos'd to fcorn,
   And wander in a ftate forlorn.

41 But he exalts the poor on high,
   And fpreads their numerous Family.
42 The Juft with Gladnefs this fhall fee,
   And wickednefs fhall filent be.

43 How few there are with care record
   Thefe wonderous dealings of the Lord!
   All wife obfervers ftill fhall find,
   That God is infinitely kind,

Pfalm CX.

(*As the* 100 *Pfalm.*)

1 THus fpake the Lord unto his Son,
   Sit thou advanc'd on my right hand,
   Till all thy conquered Foes fhall crouch,
   And wait their doom from thy command.

2 From Sion fhall thy word go forth,
   Which like a Sceptre thou fhalt fway ;

To

To bring the stubborn under rule,
And make them willingly obey.

3 Thy Conquests shall be great that day,
The numerous Converts thou shalt view,
Shall make an Army that exceeds
The Crystal drops of Morning dew.

4 The Lord hath all his Truth engag'd
By Oath, which he can never break,
To make thee an eternal Priest,
Of th' Order of Melchizedeck.

5 And when he's rais'd to his Throne.
Proud Monarchs that oppose his Reign
6 Shall fall, and all the wicked World
That will not stoop to him, be slain.

7 While he pursues this work, he'll stoop
To mean refreshments in the way;
But with a glorious reward,
God will his sufferings repay.

Psalm CXI.

1 MY Souls best Pow'rs I will engage,
And with affection join
In those Assemblies, where the Saints
To praise the Lord combine.
2 They that contemplate thy great works,
Will soon with pleasure see
3 Thy pow'r how glorious it is,
How great thy purity.

H 3

4 The

4 The wonders of thy Providence
　　They'll often call to mind;
　With gratefull hearts proclaim, that God,
　　Is gratious and kind.
5 How in the Wilderneſs he gave
　　Food with a liberal hand;
6 And made his people to poſſeſs
　　The Heathens pleaſant land.

7 Faithfull and juſt are all his works,
　　His word is no leſs ſure;
8 When once his promiſe is engag'd,
　　Performance is ſecure.
9 Iſrael, from ſlavery redeem'd,
　　His Holineſs did know;
　Their Foes the Terrour of thy Name
　Felt in their overthrow.

10 To fear the Lord true wiſedom is,
　　And he that ſtrives to pleaſe
　His Maker, underſtands him beſt,
　　Whoſe praiſe ſhall never ceaſe.

Pſalm CXII.

(As the 100 Pſalm.)

1 BLeſt is the Man that fears the Lord,
　　Whoſe pleaſure 'tis to do his will;
2 His Seed ſhall be renown'd on Earth,
　His happy race ſhall flouriſh ſtill.
3 His Houſe with plenty ſhall be fill'd;
　And as his wealth and ſtores increaſe,

His

His Bounty is enlarg'd; no fear
Of future want do's make it less,

4 When troubles fall unto his share,
They'll in his greater comfort end;
What kindness God on him bestows,
The same to others he'll extend.

5 He lends assistance to the poor,
Discreetly orders all his way;
6 Nothing shall move this Righteous Man,
Or make his Memory decay.

7 No news of threatning dangers can
His confidence in God displace;
8 He with undaunted courage looks
His Foes securely in the face.

9 God his diffusive Charity
With sutable rewards will crown;
Not onely those above bestow,
But honour here and great renown.

10 Mean While the wicked shall repine
With indignation at his Bliss;
And melt away with grief, to see
This Man obtain, what they shall miss.

Psalm CXII.

(Another Metre.)

1 O Happy man that fears the Lord,
And joys to do his will;

2 His Seed ſhall be renown'd on Earth,
   His race ſhall flouriſh ſtill.

3 His Houſe with plenty ſhall be fill'd;
   And as his ſtores increaſe,
His bounty is enlarg'd; no fear
   Of want do's make it leſs.

4 When troubles fall unto his ſhare,
   They'll in his comfort end;
what kindneſs God on him beſtows,
   To others he'll extend.

5 He lends aſſiſtance to the poor,
   Diſcreetly guides his way;

6 Nothing ſhall move this man, or make
   His Memory decay.

7 His Truſt in God, no threatning News
   Of Danger can diſplace:

8 He with undaunted Courage looks
   His En'mies in the Face.

9 God his diffuſive Charity
   With great Rewards will Crown;
Both thoſe above beſtow, and here
   Honour and great Renown.

10 Mean while the wicked ſhall repine
   With envy at his Bliſs;
Conſume with grief, to ſee this Man
   Obtain, what they ſhall miſs.

Pſalm CXIII.

1 YE Servants of th' Eternal King,
   To God your chearfull praiſes ſing,

2 Who-

2 Whose Name be blest for evermore.
3 His goodness over all is great,
Where e'er the Sun do's rise or set;
Since all are blest, let all adore.
4 O'er all the Earth the Lord do's reign,
And Heav'n's too narrow to contain
His Glories that are infinite.
5 Let not poor borrow'd greatness dare
With his Perfections to compare,
Who dwells in uncreated Light.
6 He condescends so far, to know
Th' affairs of Mortals here below,
As well as those in Heav'n above.
7 To shew how he o'er all things sways,
He from the Dust the poor do's raise,
And from his vile estate remove:
8 From thence advances him on high
To unexpected Dignity,
And sets him in a Royal Throne.
9 When Age and Nature both despair,
He makes the Barren Womb to bear:
O therefore praise this God alone.

Psalm CXV.

(*As the* 100 *Psalm.*)

NOt unto us, Lord, not to us
But to thy Name the praise we owe;
To thy free goodness and thy Truth,
The Springs whence all our Blessings flow.

2 Why ſhould the Heathen ask in ſcorn,
   Where is the God whom you adore ?
3 In Heav'n he Reigns; but do's on Earth
   What e'er his will ordain'd before.

4 Silver and Gold their Idols are,
   And all their worth derive from thence;
   With no Divinity inſpir'd,
   Since they are void of Life or ſenſe.

5 For tho' the Maker forms an Eye,
6 A Mouth, or any other part;
7 He cannot give them ſight or breath,
   Nor lively motion by his Art.

8 Fond men! to think your Hands can make
   A God, to which our Knees ſhould bow;
   You truſt what cannot help it ſelf;
   Statues have ſenſe as much as you.

Part. II.

9 All ye that know and fear the Lord,
   In him repoſe your confidence;
10 With all that at his Altars wait,
11 He is their helper and defence.

12 God has been mindfull of our good,
   And thoſe that fear him ſtill will bleſs;
13 His Mercies both to ſmall and great,
14 And to their Race ſhall never ceaſe.

15 O happy ſtate thus to be bleſt
   By him that made both Earth and Heav'n;
16 His Throne in Heav'n is plac'd, the Earth
   In kindneſs he to Man has giv'n.

17 The

17 The silent Grave cannot declare
  Thy wonders, nor proclaim thy praise;
18 We'll now begin that Blessed work,
  Which shall continue all our days.

Psalm CXV.

(*Another Metre.*)

1 LOrd, not to us, but to thy Name
    We give the praise we owe;
  To thy free goodness and thy truth,
    Whence all our Blessings flow.
2 Why should the Heathen ask us, where's
    The God whom you adore?
3 In Heav'n he Reigns, but do's on Earth
    What he ordain'd before.

4 Silver and Gold their Idols are,
    Their worth derive from thence;
  With no Divinity inspir'd,
    Since void of Life or sense.
5 For tho' the Maker forms an Eye,
6   A Mouth, or other part;
7 He cannot give them sight or breath,
    Motion, or Life, by Art.

8 Fond men! With Hands to make a God
    To which our Knees should bow;
  You trust what cannot help it self;
    Statues have sense like you.

Part.

Part. II.

9 All ye that know the Lord, in him
     Repose your confidence:
10 Ye that attend his Altars, trust
     This helper and defence.
12 God has remembred us and those
     That fear him still will bless;
13 To you and yours, both small and great,
14   His mercies ne'er shall cease,
15 Oh happy! to be blest by him
     That made both Earth and Heav'n;
16 His Throne's in Heav'n, the Earth to Man
     In kindness he has given.
17 The Grave thy wonders cannot show,
     Nor celebrate thy praise;
18 We'll now adore thy sacred name,
     And bless thee all our days.

Psalm CXVI.

(*As the* 100 *Psalm.*)

1 SInce God so tender a regard
     To all my poor requests did give;
2 My best affections he shall have,
   And best Devotions, whilst I live.

3 Assayl'd with grief and pains, that seem'd
   The sad Forerunners of the Grave;
4 To thee I made request: O Lord,
   My life from threatning danger save.

5 Nor

5 Nor did I cry to God in vain,
  Nor did his Mercy come too late;
6 But when my skill was at a loss,
  His kindness rais'd my low estate.

7 God and thy self, my Soul, enjoy
  In quiet rest, freed from thy tears;
8 Who sav'd thy Life, upheld thy steps,
  And dry'd up all thy falling tears.

9 I still shall live and praise thy name,
10 Thus did I speak, and thus believ'd;
11 Tho' in distress I rashly said,
   All men will lie, and I'm deceiv'd.

12 What shall I render to the Lord,
   For all the kindness he has shown?
13 I'll humbly offer him my praise,
   And thankfully his favours own.

14 The solemn payment of the vows
   I made to God, shall be my care;
15 Who sav'd me from approaching death,
   And shew'd my Life to him was dear.

16 By all engagements, Lord, I'm thine,
   Thy Servant whom that hast set free;
   The very Bonds that thou hast loos'd
   Shall tie me faster unto thee.

Psalm CXVI.

(*Another Metre*)

1 GOD that so gratious a regard
   To my requests did give;

2 Shall

2 Shall have my choicest Love, and best
    Devotions whilst I live.

3 Assayl'd with grief and pains that seem'd
    Forerunners of the Grave,

4 To thee I cry'd: O Lord, my life
    From threatning danger save.

5 Nor did I cry in vain; nor did
    His Mercy come too late,

6 But when my skill was at a loss,
    He rais'd my low estate.

7 God and thy self, my Soul, enjoy
    Quiet and free from fears;

8 Who sav'd thy life, upheld thy steps,
    And dry'd up all thy tears.

9 I still shall live to praise thee; thus

10   I spake and thus believ'd;

11 Tho' once I rashly said, all men
    Will lye, and I'm deceiv'd.

12 What shall I render, Lord, for all
    The kindness thou hast shown?

13 Praises I'll offer, and with thanks
    Will all thy favours own.

14 The payment of the vows I made
    To God, shall be my care:

15 Who saved me from death, and shew'd
    My life to him was dear.

16 By all engagement I am thine,
    Thy Servant, Lord, I'll be;
    The bonds that thou hast loos'd, shall tye
    Me faster unto thee.

Psalm CXVII.

1 LEt all the Nations of the World
  Their great Creator praise;
And all its scattered people joyn
  His mighty Name to raise.
2 Whose kindness towards us is great,
  His Mercies ever sure;
Then let our praises like his Truth,
  For ever still endure.

Psalm CXVIII.

1 O Praise the Lord, whom Ages past
  Have known to be so kind;
Whose mercies will continue sure
  To Ages still behind.
2 Let all his people, and his Priests
3   That in his House attend;
4 With all that fear the Lord, proclaim,
  His mercies have no end.

5 Bear thou thy part with them, my Soul,
  God's goodness to express;
Who heard my Pray'r, and set me free
  When I was in distress,
6 I need not fear what Man can do,
  When God is my defence:
9 Rather in him than greatest Kings
  I'll put my confidence.

15 The

15 The joyfull voice of Triumph fills
    The dwellings of the Just;
16 His Pow'r do's mighty things for them
    That in his Goodness trust.
17 I hope to live and praise his works
    Ev'n to my latest Breath,
18 Who tho' he has chastiz'd me sore,
    Has sav'd me still from death.

Part. II.

21 I'll praise thee, who hast heard my Pray'rs;
    And tho' thou wast before
My gratious God, art now become
    My pow'rfull Saviour.
22 The stone which by the Builders deem'd
    Unfit, aside was thrown;
Is chosen and prefer'd to be
    The Head and Corner Stone.

23 This is the work of God alone,
    By us with wonder seen;
24 This is the day the Lord hath made,
    And we'll rejoice therein.
25 We'll joyn our Acclamations,
    And loud Hosanna's sing;
Wishing prosperity may wait
    On him that is our King.

26 Blest Saviour! that from God to us
    On this kind errand came.
We welcome thee; and bless all those
    That spread thy Glorious Fame.

17 Thou,

17 Thou, Lord, haſt mercifully ſhin'd
   On us with Light and Grace;
And at thine Altar we'll preſent
   Our Sacrifice of praiſe.

28 Thou art my God, my joyfull tongue
   Shall ever ſing thy praiſe;
Thou art my God, and I on high
   Thy glorious name will raiſe.
29 Let all with thankfulneſs proclaim
   That God is good and kind;
Whoſe mercies, which have ever been,
   Good men ſhall ever find.

Pſalm CXIX.

1 BLeſt is the Man, whoſe blameleſs life
   The Law of God directs;
2 Who keeps his Precepts, and whoſe heart
   To ſerve the Lord affects.
3 They never wilfully tranſgreſs,
   Who to theſe paths repair;
4 Thou, Lord, haſt charged us, to keep
   All thy Commands with care.

5 O by thy Grace ſo guide my ways
   Never from thine to ſwerve;
6 Nothing ſhall ſhame my confidence,
   Whilſt I thy Laws obſerve;
7 I'll praiſe thee better, when I'm more
   Inſtructed in thy fear:

I   8 To

8 To serve thee I resolve: O give
   Me grace to persevere.

9 But how shall youth, so prone to vice,
   Govern their Manners, Lord?
By heedfull listning to the wise
   Directions of thy word.
10 Sincerely I have begg'd thy Grace,
   O keep me close to thee.
11 I've treasur'd up thy word, that I
   Might not a Sinner be.

Part. II.

13 My high esteem of all thy Laws
   I have declar'd around;
14 Herein my joy surpasses his
   That has a Treasure found.
18 Open my Eyes that I may see
   The wonders of thy Law.
19 Who in my Pilgrimage, from hence
   Must Light and Comfort draw.

30 I've chose thy Truths to be my Guide,
   Thy Law my Rule have made:
32 I'll run the way of thy Commands,
   Since thou hast made me glad.
34 Lord, give me a discerning mind,
   And knowledge of thy will;
Then, what thy sacred Law enjoins,
   I'll heartily fulfill.

36 Incline my heart to thy Commands,
   Whilst others riches prize;
                37From

37 From the vain pleasures of this World,
   Lord, turn away mine Eyes.
To practise goodness, let my Love
   And quick desires appear;
38 Make good thy word to him, that is
   Devoted to thy fear.

Part. III.

57 Thou art my Portion, and thy word
   I count to me most dear;
58 Thy promis'd mercy and thy Love
   Before this World prefer.
59 My former wand'rings I review'd;
   And then without delay
Resolv'd to change my course, and turn
   Into thy safer way.

67 Whilst I was prosp'rous, from thy paths
   Too soon I turn'd aside;
But by thy chastisements reduc'd,
   Thy Precepts were my guide.
68 Thou, Lord, art in thy Nature good,
   And dost all good afford;
By my afflictions make me more
   Obedient to thy word.

73 Thy hands have made and fashion'd me,
   With Wisedom me endue.
And by the knowledge of thy Laws,
   Lord, form my Soul anew.
75 I know thy Judgments righteous are,
   And all my troubles just:

37 Lord,

76 Lord, let thy mercy comfort me
    For in thy word I trust.

Part. IV.

89 For ever, like the Heavens, Lord,
    Thy word is setled fast;
90 As firmly as the Earth, thy Truth
    Do's to all Ages last.
91 These all in their appointed course
    Continue to this Day:
    And all like ready Servants stand
    Thine Orders to obey.

92 Had not thy Truth been my support,
    Thy Law been my delight,
    Under the pressure of my woes,
    I' had sunk and perisht quite.
96 Of all perfection here below
    I soon discern an end;
    But thy large Precepts to all times
    And states of life extend.

97 O how I love thy Law? it is
    My daily exercise;
98 This study makes me wiser far
    Than all mine Enemies;
103 Honey no sweetness do's afford,
    Like what thy words create;
104 From thence I learn the flatt'ring sweets,
    Of every sin to hate.

Part.

Part. V.

105 Thy word is to my life a Guide,
    Unto my Paths a light;
106 I've sworn to keep thy righteous Laws,
    Which I'll perform aright.

115 Ye wicked doers that corrupt
    The World, depart from me;
From faithfull serving of my God
    Ye shall no hindrance be,

120 The sense of thy just vengeance, Lord,
    Fills me with fear and awe.

126 It's time for thee to work, for now
    Proud men despise thy Law.

132 O let thy dealings towards me,
    And mercy be the same,
Thou usest to express to those
    That love and fear thy name.

133 Order my goings in thy word,
    And my Director be;
Then no iniquity shall gain
    Dominion over me.

136 I see how Sinners break thy Laws
    By bold impieties;
This makes me sadly to lament,
    And tears o'erflow mine Eyes.

Part. VI.

137 Thy Nature, Lord, and thy Commands
    Exactly do agree;
138 Holy, and just, and true thou art,
    And such thy Preceps be.

139 This sets my zeal on fire, and makes
       My indignation rise;
  To see my Foes forget thy words,
     And thy just Laws despise.

140 Thy word from all impurer dross
       Refin'd, is my delight:

148 On this I meditate before
       The watches of the Night.   (peace

165 Those men are Crown'd with inward
       Who thy Commandments love:
  And no Temptations unto sin,
     To them a scandal prove.

167 My Soul do's all thy Precepts keep,
       And Testimonies prise;

168 For all my actions naked are
     To thine All-seeing Eyes.

176 Like a lost Sheep I've gone astray,
       But now to thee I come;
  Thy Precepts I resolve t'obey,
     Lord, bring thy servant home.

Psalm CXXI.

1 I'LL lift mine Eyes unto the Hills,
       And thence will look for aid:

2 Vain thought! it's God alone can help,
     Which Earth and Heaven made.

3 He will sustain thy weaker pow'rs
       With his Almighty Arm;

4 And keep thee with unwearied care
     From all surprising harm.

                                5 The

5 The Lord's Protection, like a Shade,
　　Will be thy sure Defence;
6 Nor Sun nor Moon shall hurt thee with
　　Malignant influence.
7 From harm thy Body he'll protect,
　　Preserve thy Soul from sin:
8 Will prosper thy Designs abroad,
　　And bless thy coming in,

Psalm CXXIII.

1 O Thou that in a glorious Throne
　　Art plac'd above the Skies!
To thee for succour I direct
　　Mine heart, and lift mine Eyes.
2 No Servant by his Lord chastis'd
　　With more submission stands:
Nor Maids with greater Duty wait
　　Their Mistresses Commands.

Than we that justly undergo
　　The Discipline of God,
Wait for a mercifull release,
　　When he'll remove his Rod.
3 Have mercy, Lord, on us, whose hope
　　In thy Compassion lies;
And, whom insulting Foes do scorn,
　　Lord, do not thou despise.
4 For our deprest estate now gives
　　Advantage to their Pride:
And they that live in wealth and ease,
　　Our miseries deride.

Psalm

Pſalm CXXIV.

1 HAD not the Lord our cauſe eſpous'd,
  His people now may ſay ;
2 Had not the Lord engag'd his pow'r
  To ſuccour us that day.
  When wicked men, with cruel wrath
  Inflam'd, againſt us roſe ;
3 Too feeble all our pow'rs had been
  Their fury to oppoſe.

4 To their devouring Jaws our life
  Had been an eaſy prey ;
5 Their rage, like an impetuous ſtream,
  Had ſwept us quite away.
6 Bleſt be the Lord, that choſe this way
  His mercy to enhance ;
  Then when our dangers loudeſt call'd
  To ſend Deliverance.

7 We lay like poor entangled Birds,
  Caught in the Fowlers Net :
  God's power broke the ſnare, and we
  At Liberty were ſet.
8 Since all our help lies in his name
  That Earth and Heaven made :
  Our future hopes ſhall all depend
  On his Almighty aid.

Pſalm CXXV.

(*As the* 100 *Pſalm.*)

1 THey that in God their Confidence
  Repoſe, and him their Fortreſs make,

Re-

Remain unmov'd, like Sions Mount,
Which Storms and Tempests never shake.

2 Jerusalem with Hills begirt,
Derives great safety from that fence;
Good Men much more from Angels guard,
And God's surrounding Providence.

3 The wickeds Pow'r shall not too long
Oppress the good, and vex their peace;
Lest the Temptation prove so strong,
They imitate their wickedness.

4 Bless those that are sincerely good;
5 And when thy vengeance shall come down,
Rebellious Sinners to destroy,   (crown.
Then, Lord, with peace the Righteous

Psalm CXXV.

(Another Metre.)

1 THey that repose their trust in God,
    And him their Fortress make,
Remain unmov'd, like Sions Mount
    Which Tempests never shake.

2 Jerusalem with Hills begirt,
    Is safe by this defence;
Good men are more secure from God's
    Surrounding Providence.

3 The wickeds pow'r shall not too long
    Oppress and vex their peace;
Lest, through discouragement, they prove
    Like them in wickedness.

I 5   4 Bless

4 Bless all the truely good; and when
  Thy vengeance shall come down
 Proud Sinners to destroy; then, Lord,
  With Peace the Righteous crown.

Psalm CXXVI.

(*As the* 100 *Psalm.*)

1 WHen God from Bondage set us free,
  It seem'd a strange and pleasant dream;
2 Our Mouth was fill'd with laughter then,
 To tell this news was all our Theam,

 This great and unexpected change
 Forced the Heathens to confess
3 The wonders of that day; let us
 The same with greather joy express.

 Great are thy Mercies shewn to us;
4 Lord, perfect what thou hast begun;
 'Twill be like welcome show'rs to ground
 That's partched with the scortching Sun.

5 We wait with patience, Lord, till thou
 All nedfull Blessings dost restore;
 And hope our former tears will make
 Our after-joys to be the more.

6 So he that in prepared ground
 His scattered handfulls sadly leaves,
 Will shout at Harvest, when he sees
 That Seed become a Load of Sheaves.
        Psalm

Psalm CXXVI.

(*Another Metre.*)

1 WHen God redeem'd our Captive State,
    It seem'd a pleasant dream :
2 Our Mouth was fill'd with Laughter then,
    And joy was all our Theam.
This mercy so unlook'd for , mov'd
    The Heathens to confess
3 The wonders of that Day, let us
    With joy the same express.

Great are thy Mercies shewn to us:
4   Lord, perfect what's begun :
'Twill be like welcome show'rs to ground
    Partch'd with the scortching Sun.
5 We wait with Patience, Lord, till thou
    All good to us restore;
And hope our former tears will make
    Our after-joys the more.

6 So he that in prepared ground
    His scattered handfulls leaves ;
Will shout at Harvest, when that Seed
    Becomes a Load of Sheaves.

Psalm CXXVII.

(*As the* 100 *Psalm.*)

1 IF God be not the Architect,
    Men strive in vain a House t'erect :

Un-

Unless the Lord the City keep,
The watchfull Guards as well may sleep.

2 Your Labours with the rising Sun
Begin, and last when Day is done:
T'avoid that Poverty you dread,
With carefulness you eat your Bread.

But all in vain: by Heaven blest
You may enjoy both wealth and rest;
3 A numerous Race and fruitfull Womb
As God's rewards to Goodness come:

4 Their Parents strength and Glory are,
Like Arrows to a Man of War:
5 Well furnished with these supplies,
A Man may dare his Enemies.

Psalm CXXVIII.

1 BLest is the Man, whose fear of God
Is by obedience shown:
2 Plenty thy Labours shall reward,
And good success shall crown.
3 Thy fruitfull Wife, like a fair Vine
With Clusters shall abound;
Whose Children like green olive Plants,
Thy Table shall surround.

4 Such Blessings to thy House shall fall
When God's thy chiefest fear;
5 Thou in the publick joy and good
Shalt have the greatest share.
6 A numerous Race from thee deriv'd
Thy lengthned Age shall see;

And

And, the great wish of all good Men,
The Lands prosperity.

Psalm CXXX.

(*As the* 100 *Psalm.*)

1 PLung'd in the Confines of despair,
    To God I cry'd with fervent Pray'r;
2 O lend to me a gratious Ear;
Not sunk so low but thou canst hear.

3 Should'st thou against each evil deed
In strict severity proceed,
Who would be able to abide
Thy censure, and be justify'd?

4 But thou forgiveness dost proclaim,
That men may turn and fear thy name.
5 To thy rich Grace, O Lord, we fly,
    And on thy promises rely.

6 My Soul less brooks thy seeming stay,
ThanGuards that watch th' approach of day.
7 O therefore let the good and just
In God alone repose their trust.

The frailty of our state he knows;
His plenteous Mercy ever flows.
8 To humble Souls he gratious is,
And pardons what they've done amiss.

Psalm CXXXI.

1 LOrd, I have no aspiring thoughts,
    Nor Eyes that lofty are;

Nor

Nor meddle with the things advanc'd,
 Above my lower Sphere.
2 But humble and resign'd I lie
 Compos'd to silent rest;
Mine as a Child's behaviour is,
 Wean'd from his Mothers Breast.

3 Let pious Souls no more admire
 The Worlds deceitfull shows;
But with an undisturbed mind
 In God their trust repose.

Psalm CXXXIII.

(*As the* 100 *Psalm.*)

1 O Blest Societies on Earth,
 Resembling that of Heav'n above!
Where Brethren peacefully unite
In sweet accord and hearty Love.

2 It's like the pretious Ointment pour'd
 On Aaron's confecrated head;
Which first ran down his face, and thence
Unto his costly vesture spread.

3 Like dews that visit every Hill,
 Or as the fruitfull show'rs of rain;
Tho' first on higher grounds they fall,
Descend, and water all the plain.

Innumerable comforts meet,
Where Love and Amity abound;

Their

Their Souls are fill'd with inward peace,
Their prosperous State with blessing
   crown'd.

Psalm CXXXIII.

(*another Metre*)

1 O Happy Companies on Earth,
  Resembling Heav'n above;
Where Brethren peacefully unite,
  In sweet Accord and Love.
2 It's like the pretious Ointment pour'd
  Upon the High Priest's Head;
Which first ran down his Face, and thence
  Unto his Garments spread.

3 Like dews that visit every Hill,
  Or fruitfull showrs of rain;
Tho' first on higher grounds they fall,
  Thence water all the plain.
Innumerable comforts meet,
  Where mutual Love is found;
Their Souls are fill'd with inward peace,
  Their State with blessing crown'd.

Psalm CXXXIV.

(*As the* 100 *Psalm.*)

1 YE Servants of th' Eternal King,
  Who early at his Temple wait,

       And

And there your late attendance give,
See that his Name ye celebrate.

2 And, as that Holy place requires,
Pure hands in your Devotions raise;
To all your other offerings joyn
The gratefull Sacrifice of praise.

3 God the Great Maker of the World,
As great in Goodness as in pow'r,
Give gratious Answers to thy Pray'rs.
And bless his people every hour.

Psalm CXXXIV.

(*Another Metre.*)

1 YE Servants of the Lord above,
     Who at his Temple wait;
See that before the rising Sun
     His Name ye celebrate·

2 And in that Holy place, pure hands
     In your Devotions raise;
To all your other offerings joyn
     The Sacrifice of praise.

3 The Lord that made the World, as great
     In goodness as in pow'r,
Give Ear to thy requests, and bless
     His people every hour.

Psalm

Psalm CXXXV.

1 YE Servants of th' Almighty Lord,
    That Heav'n and Earth did frame;

2 Who at his House and Altar wait,
    Praise ye his Glorious Name.

3 O let the Goodness of the Lord
    Your best affections raise;
Your inward Pleasure will increase,
    Together with your praise.

5 In him do all perfections meet,
    His Greatness knows no bound;
What e'er by other Gods is claim'd,
    In him alone is found.

6 His Pow'r created all at first,
    His Pleasure rules them still;
His uncontrolled mind the Heav'n,
    The Earth and Seas fulfill.

7 By undiscerned force he makes
    The vapours to arise,   (quench'd,
Which frame the Clouds, where fire un-
    Mingled with water lies.
From thence the dreadfull Lightnings burst,
    And Rains are poured down;
He brings his boysterous Winds and Storms
    From Treasuries unknown.

13 Supported by thy Glorious Works,
    Thy Fame can never die;
But thy Memorial shall endure
    To all Eternity.

K   Psalm

Psalm CXXXV.

(Another Metre. As the 148 Psalm.)

1 YE Servants of the Lord
    That Heav'n and Earth did frame;
2 Who at his Altars wait,
Praise ye his glorious name.
3   His goodness doth
        To this invite;
        His praise will give
        The best delight.

5 In him all Glories meet;
His Greatness knows no bound;
What other Gods do claim,
In him is onely found.
6   Who as at first
        He all things made,
        Still rules o'er all,
        By all obey'd.

7 All things in Heav'n above
Are subject to his will;
The Earth and Seas below
His pleasure do fulfill.
        At his Command,
        From the Worlds end,
        Vapours to frame
        The Clouds ascend.

Lightnings from thence burst out,
And Rains are poured down;

He

He brings his boyst'rous Winds
From Treasuries unknown.
13   Thy Name and thy
      Memorial,
      For ever, Lord,
      Continue shall.

Psalm CXXXVI.

(as the 148 Psalm.)

1 GIve thanks unto the Lord
    That is so kind and good;
Whose mercies firmly last,
As they have ever stood.
2   To this great King
      All Gods do bow,
3   Angels above
      And Pow'rs below.

4 His works our wonder raise;
5 The Heav'ns his wisedom made;
6 And he th'out-stretched Earth
Above the Waters laid.
7   He made the Sun
8   The Days great Light,
9   The Moon and Stars
      To rule the Night.

10 Egypts first-born be smote,
11 And by his pow'rfull hand
12 He brake off Israels Yoke,
  And brought them from that Land.

K 2

His

His Mercies shown
To Ages past,
Eternally
Shall spring and last.

13 The parted Sea made way
14 For Israel to pass;
15 There the pursuing Host
Of Pharaoh drowned was.
16   His people through
        The Desart led,
        By Miracles
        Were daily fed.

17 18 Kings that oppos'd their way,
19 20 Sihon and Og he smote;
21   And made their fruitfull land
22   Fall to his peoples Lot.
        His Mercies shown
        To Ages past,
        Eternally
        Shall spring and last.

23 He sav'd us when our State
24 Was low and sore opprest;
25 Food to all flesh he gives,
26 The God of Heav'n be blest.
        Whose Mercies shown
        To Ages past,
        Eternally
        Shall spring and last.

Psalm

Psalm CXXXVIII.

1 TO magnify the Lord, my Soul
 Thy best affections raise;
Angels shall hear my Songs, and be
 The Partners of my praise.

2 Within thy Church thy Constant truth
 And goodness I'll proclaim;
These raise my wonder, and advance
 The Glories of thy Name.

3 In my distress to thee I cry'd,
 And thou my Pray'r didst hear;
Thou didst support me with thy strength,
 And with thy comforts cheer.

4 Kings shall thy promis'd goodness know,
 And take occasion thence

5 To praise thy Mercy, and admire
 Thy ways of Providence.

6 God from his high and Glorious Throne
 The lowly views and owns;
But scorns the proud, and on their height
 With indignation frowns.

7 Thy former kindnesses prevent
 My fears, when in distress;
Thy hand shall save me from my Foes,
 Thy Pow'r their wrath repress.

8 Thy never-failing Goodness will
 Complete what is begun;
O never suffer thine own work,
 Nor me to be undone.

K 3   Psalm

Psalm CXXXIX.

(*As the 100 Psalm.*)

1 LOrd, when I have to doe with thee,
    In vain I seek to be conceal'd:
2 Thou know'st me perfectly, to thee
    My very thoughts are all reveal'd.

3 Both when I sit and when I rise,
    My walking and my lying down;
4 To thee my works and all my words,
    Better than to my self, are known.

5 On every side within the reach
    Of thine encircling Arm I lie;
6 Whose force I neither can resist,
    Nor scape the notice of thine Eye.

7 Whither can I retire, and find
    A place where God do's never come?
8 His Glories I should meet in Heav'n;
    His Pow'r, had I in Hell a room.

9 Could I remove to th' utmost Sea
    Wing'd with the swiftest Morning ray;
10 Thy hand that thither must support
    My flight, would my abode betray.

11 If o'er my sins I think to draw
    The blackest Curtains of the Night;
12 All will be clear to thee; for what
    We darkness call, to thee is Light.

13 My inmost Reins by thee possess'd,
    With all th' affections seated there;

To thee, that made'st those hidden Springs
Within the Womb, must needs appear.

Part. II.

14 In all thy works, O Lord, see
   The Footsteps of thy wond'rous skill;
   And to excite my praise, I find
   Within my self more wonders still.

15 Unseen by all, when form'd within
   The dark recesses of the Womb;
   Before the fine Embroidery
   Of parts was to perfection come;

16 In that rude Mass, thou didst discern
   The Daily growth of every part;
   And what th'Eternal mind had fram'd,
   Was copied out with curious art.

17 Lord, I admire the various thoughts
   And the wise Counsels of thy mind;
   Their sum is infinite; yet all
   Are dear to me, because they're kind.

18 Their number's greater than the sand;
   Which whilst my busy thoughts run o'er,
   I sleep; and find when I awake,
   I'm onely where I was before.

23 Lord, since my thoughts accuse me not
   Of living in a false disguise;
   I'm less afraid to undergo
   The Tryal of thy peircing Eyes.

K 4   24 Search

14 Search me; and if thou see'st that I
   Unwillingly have done amiss,
   Correct my errours, and reduce
   My wandrings to the way of Bliss.

Psalm CXXXIX.

(Another Metre)

1 WHen, Lord, I deal with thee, in vain
   I seek to be conceal'd.
2 Thou know'st me perfectly, my thoughts
   To thee are all reveal'd.
3 Both when I sit and when I rise,
   Walking and lying down;
4 My works and words, better to thee
   Than to my self are known.

5 Ever within the reach of thine
   Encircling Arm I lie;
6 Whose force I neither can resist,
   Nor scape thy piercing Eye.
7 In vain, where God do's never come,
   I seek to find a Seat;
8 For plac'd in Hell, thy Pow'r; in Heav'n,
   Thy Glories I should meet.

9 Could I remove to th' utmost Sea,
   Wing'd with the Mornings Ray;
10 Thy hand that must support my flight,
   Would my abode betray.
11 If o'er my sins I think to draw
   The Curtains of the Night;

12 All's

12 All's clear to thee, for what we call
   Darkness, to thee is Light.

13 My Reins by thee possess'd, with all
   Th' affections seated there,
   To thee, that mad'st within the Womb
   Those hidden Springs, appear.

Part. II.

14 In all thy, works, O Lord, I see
   Footsteps of wond'rous skill ;
   And in my self, t' excite my praise,
   I find more wonders still.
15 When form'd unseen, within the dark
   Recesses of the Womb ;
   Before th' Embroydery of Parts
   Was to perfection come.

16 In that rude Mass, thou didst discern
   The growth of every part ;
   And what th' Eternal mind had fram'd,
   Was drawn with curious art.
17 Lord, I admire the various thoughts,
   And Counsels of thy mind ;
   Their sum is infinite, yet dear
   To me, because they're kind.

18 Their Number's greater than the Sand ;
   Which whilst my thoughts run o'er,
   I sleep; and find when I awake,
   I'm where I was before.
23 Lord, since my thoughts accuse me not
   T' have liv'd in false disguise ;

I'm less afraid to undergo
   The Tryal of thine Eyes.
24 Search me, and where unwillingly
   'Thou see'st I've done amiss;
  Correct, and lead my wandring steps
   Into the way of Bliss.

Psalm CXLIII.

1 REgard the fervent Pray'rs I make,
   The hopes I have in thee;
And, Lord, according to thy Truth
   And Goodness answer me.
2 Let not my failings be before
   Thy strict Tribunal try'd;
For, Lord, if thou should'st be severe,
   None could be justify'd.

I'll ne'er cease asking till my Soul
   Shall thy refreshments gain;
Thy mercy which I gasp for more,
   Than thirsty ground for rain.
7 My Spirits sink while thou delay'st
   Th' assistance I would have;
If God still frown on my requests,
   'Twill sink me to the Grave.

8 The Night is witness of my tears
   As well as trust in thee;
O let the joyfull Morning tell
   Thy kindness towards me.
Lord be my Guide, that I may find
   The way where I should go:

9 Be

9 Be thou my refuge from their pow'r
That seek my overthrow.

10 Teach me, my God, to do thy will;
And let thy spirit of Love,
Conduct me in the paths that lead
To happiness above.

11 Revive my fainting Soul, thy Name
And honour to advance;
Thy faithfulness will brightly shine
In my deliverance.

Psalm CXLV.

1 I Will extoll thy sacred Name,
Thou King of Saints and God of Love:

2 I'll bless thee daily now, 'twill be
My work eternally above.

3 Our praises should be high like thee,
Whose greatness all our thoughts exceeds;

4 And what one Age do's not confine,
The next shall tell thy mighty deeds.

5 I'll shew the glories of thy State,
And thy amazing works proclaim:

6 All men that hear my Songs of praise,
Shall gladly joyn to do the same.

7 And like the unexhausted Springs
Of mercy, so their joys shall flow;
Their tongues thy faithfulness shall sing,
And thine abundant goodness show.

8 Thou,

8 Thou, Lord, art full of Grace and Love,
   To anger flow, but glad to spare;
9 To all thy Creatures thou art kind,
   O'er all thy tender mercies are.

10 Thou, Lord, from all these works of thine
   Some thankfull Tribute doft receive;
   But where their powers fail, thy praise
   Among the Saints shall ever live.

11 These happy Subjects to declare
   Thy Kingdoms glory never cease;
12 That Men the Triumphs of thy Grace
   May know, and all thy Pow'r confess.

Part. II.

13 Thy Kingdom, Lord shall ever stand,
   Tho' often undermin'd in vain;
14 Oppressed goodness is sustain'd
   By thee; when falling, rais'd again.

15 All Creatures do expect from thee
   Supplies of seasonable food;
16 Thy open-handed bounty fills
   Their longings with desired good.

17 God's Goodness and Fidelity
   In all his Ways and Works appear;
18 He gives kind answers to their Pray'rs
   That call on him, and are sincere.

19 There's none that fear him need complain
   That they in vain have sought his aid;
   He hears their cries, when in distress;
   And saves them when they are afraid.

20 God's

20 God's Preservation shall reward
   The Good Man's Duty and his Love;
   But the bold crimes of wicked men,
   Shall at the length their ruine prove.

21 Mean while my tongue shall be employ'd
   Thy chearfull praises to proclaim;
   Let all the World adore thy pow'r,
   And ever bless thy Holy Name.

Psalm CXLV.

(*Another Metre.*)

1 THY sacred name I will advance,
    My King, and God of Love;
2 I'll bless thee now, 'twill be my work
    Eternally above.
3 Our praises should be high like thee,
    Whose Greatness all exceeds;
4 One Age t' another shall declare,
    And praise thy mighty deeds.

5 I'll shew the Glories of thy State,
    Thy wondrous works proclaim;
6 All men that hear my Songs of praise,
    Shall joyn to do the same.
7 And as thy Mercy ever springs,
    So shall their comforts flow;
   Their tongues thy faithfulness shall sing,
    And thy great goodness show.

8 Thou, Lord, art slow to wrath, but full
    Of Love, and glad to spare;

9 To

9 To all thy Creatures kind, o'er all
   Thy tender Mercies are.
10 Some thankfull Tribute, Lord, from all
   Thy works thou dost receive;
   But where they fail, thy praise among
   The Saints shall ever live.

11 Thy Kingdoms Glory to declare
   These Subjects never cease;
12 That men thy wond'rous Grace may know,
   And all thy pow'r confess.

Part. II.

13 Thy Kingdom, Lord, shall ever stand,
   Tho' undermin'd in vain;
14 Goodness is stay'd by thee, when weak;
   When falling, rais'd again.
15 All Creatures do expect from thee
   Supplies of daily food;
16 Thy open-handed bounty fills
   All their desires with good.

17 God's Goodness and Fidelity,
   In all his ways appear;
18 He gives kind answers unto such
   As pray, and are sincere.
19 There's none that fear him need complain
   They've sought in vain his aid;
   He hears their cryes, when in distress,
   And saves them, when afraid.

20 God's care and preservation
   Rewards the good man's Love;

But

But the bold crimes of wicked men
At length their ruine prove.
21 Mean while my tongue shall be employ'd
Thy praises to proclaim;
Let all the World adore thy Pow'r,
And ever bless thy Name.

Psalm CXLVI.

1 MY Soul to praise the Highest Lord
Thy best affections raise;
2 For whilst I live my God shall be
The subject of my praise.
3 Vain are our hopes from Mighty Kings;
Whose Glories at their Death
4 Sink to the Grave, and all their thoughts
Do vanish with their Breath.

5 Happy is he, who in that God
That made the World do's trust;
6 Which World may sooner fail, than he
Cease to be good and just.
7 He rights the injur'd, and defends
The good Man's cause oppress'd;
He feeds the hungry, and by him
The Prisoners are releas'd.

8 He cures the blind, and sorrow from
Dejected Souls removes;
And by his special care protects
The Righteous whom he loves.

9 Stran-

9 Strangers and Widows he preferves,
  He do's the Orphans own;
 As for the wickeds prosperous state
  He turns it upside down.

10 This Mighty King shall ever Reign,
  As he do's ever Live;
 Let all the World he rules, to him
  Eternal praises give.

Psalm CXLVII.

(*as the* 100 *Psalm.*)

1 O Blest employment of our Lives
   To praise the God whom we adore!
 How gratefull to our selves and him!
 Nothing becomes a good man more.

2 The Lord of old the broken state
 Of Captive Israel did repair;
3 The sorrowfull and broken hearts
 He binds and heals with tender care.

4 He numbers all the Stars, and knows
 What vertue comes to us from thence;
 For 'tis from him they borrow all
 Their Lustre, and their Influence'

5 Unsearsable his wisedom is,
 His pow'r so great it knows no bounds;
6 He raises up the meek, and throws
 The stubborn Sinners to the ground.

Part.

Part. II.

7 To God your chearfull praises sing,
  Whose bounty all things do's maintain;
8 Who covers Heav'n with watry Clouds,
  And for the Earth prepares the rain.

He makes the tender Grass to grow
On Mountains which are parch'd and dry;
9 Wild Beasts are fed without our care,
  And the young Ravens when they cry.

15 All Creatures haste t'obey his word;
16 Like softest Wooll he sends the Snows:
17 His Crystal Ice like Morsels casts,
  And the Hoar-frosts like ashes strows.

None can endure his piercing cold;
18 But at his word warm winds do blow;
  Then Rocks of Ice are soon dissolv'd,
  And the congealed Waters flow.

19 All see these works: to Israel
He greater favours did afford;
The clearer knowledge of his will
And Laws they had. Praise ye the Lord.

Psalm CXLVII.

(*Another Metre.*)

1 HOw well we are employ'd, to praise
  The Lord whom we adore!

L   How

How gratefull to our selves and him!
   Nothing becomes us more.
2 The Lord of old the broken state
   Of Israel did repair;
3 The sorrowfull and broken hearts
   He heals with tender care.

4 He numbers all the Stars, and knows
   What vertue comes from thence;
For 'tis from him they borrow all
   Their Light and Influence.
5 Unsearchable his wisedom is,
   His Pow'r admits no bound:
6 He raises up the meek, and throws
   Proud Sinners to the ground,

Part. II.

7 To God your chearfull praises sing.
   That all things do's maintain:
8 Who covers Heav'n with Clouds, and for
   The Earth prepares the rain.
He makes the tender Grass to grow
   On Mountains parch'd and dry;
9 Wild Beasts need not our care, he feeds
   Young Ravens when they cry.

15 All Creatures haste t'obey his word:
16   Like Wool he sends the Snows;
17 His Crystal Ice like Morsels casts,
   Hoar-frosts like ashes strows.
None can abide his piercing cold:
18   He bids warm Winds to blow;

Then

Then Rocks of Ice diſſolve, and ſoon
  Congealed Rivers flow.

19 All ſee theſe works, to Iſrael
  More grace he did afford;
  The clearer knowledge of his will
  And Laws. Praiſe ye the Lord.

Pſalm CXLVIII.

1 To laud the Heav'nly King
    Let all their voices raiſe i
2 Ye Angels firſt begin
The great Creator's praiſe.
3   Let Sun and Moon
    And every Star
    His Glory ſhow
    That's brighter far.

4 Ye Regions of the air,
And watry Clouds that move
Within the liquid Skie,
5 Praiſe ye the Lord above;
    Whoſe pow'rfull word
    Made you to be:
6   And fix'd your bounds
    By his Decree.

7 All that the Earth do's bear:
Whales in the Depths conceal'd;
8 Lightnings, and Hail, and Snow,
Vapours to Ice congeal'd,

L 2   The

The stormy Winds
Rais'd at his will,
Which at his word
Are calm'd and still.

9 Praise him ye Mountains high,
And Hills that lower are;
Cedars with lofty heads,
And Trees that fruit do bear.

10   Beasts that in Fields
Or Pastures lye;
Both creeping things
And Fouls that fly.

11 Ye Kings that Sceptres sway,
People of meaner Birth;
Princes that rule the World,
And Judges of the Earth,

12   Let every Sex
And every Age

13   To praise the name
Of God engage.

His Glories all that shines
In Earth and Heav'n excell;
14 He special mercy show'd
T'his people Israel;
A people dear
And highly rais'd;
His Holy Name
Be ever prais'd.

Psalm

Psalm CL.

1 PRaise God within that sacred place
      Where he his Grace bestows;
   Your wondering thoughts to Heaven raise,
      Where he his Glory shows.
2 Let all his Mighty Acts of Pow'r
      Your inward Passions move;
   That your Acknowledgments may suit
      The Greatness of his Love.

3 Musicks soft notes, and louder sounds
4   Of Instruments employ
5 T'excite Devotion, and attend
      The triumphs of your joy.
6 Since all to this Creator owe
      That Breath by which they live;
   Let every thing that breaths, to him
      Their chearfull praises give.

L 3   An

An Advertisement.

Tho' all these Psalms *are to be sung to the Tunes commonly used in Churches*, yet more of them are fitted to some of those Tunes than before. Not to mention the many that may be sung as the 100 Psalm; These follovving are to be sung as the twenty fifth Psalm: viz. Psalm 25. 53. 62. 67. 70. 71. These as the Hundred and thirteenth: viz. Psalm 82. 85. 113. And these as the Hundred Forty Eighth: viz. 135. (second Metre) 136. 148.

Being also unvvilling, that an unskilfull Reader should be at any loss, or frame an uncertain sense of some fevv vvords and phrases in this Version, that are of less common use: I haue therefore added their trve Signification.

SE-

SELECT

HYMNS,

Taken out of the

NEW TESTAMENT,

And used in the

CHURCH-SERVICE.

Hymn I.

Benedictus.

(The Song of Zacharias. *Luc.* 1. 68.)

LEt Isr'els pow'rfull God and King
 Eternally be blest;
Who came from Heav'n to visit us,
 And all our Bonds releas'd.
In David's House a Saviour rais'd,
 To sit upon his Throne;
This, ever since the World began,
 His Prophets have fore-shown.

L 4

That

That he would save us from the Pow'r
  And Malice of our Foes;
The Mercy to perform that he
  T' our Fathers did difclofe.
To call to mind how he engag'd
  His Truth by Covenant;
His folemn Oath to Abraham fworn;
  That he his Grace would grant,

To ferve him without fear, from all
  Our Adverfaries free'd;
And to continue all our days
  A Holy Life to lead.
And thou bleft Child to this high Lord
  Shalt have a Prophet's place;
Like a preparing Harbinger
  Shalt go before his face.

By the Remiffion of Mens fins
  To make Salvation known.
God's tender mercy, when this Sun
  Arofe, to all was fhown.
He will our fad and difmal ftate
  With Light and Comfort blefs;
And Guide our feet into the way
  Of Peace and Happinefs.

Hymn

Hymn II.

Magnificat.

(As the 100 Pſalm.)

(*The Song of the Bl. Virgin. Luc.* 1, 46.)

MY Soul doth magnify the Lord,
In thee my ſpirit do's rejoice
My God and Saviour; who deſerv'ſt
The Praiſes of my heart and voice.

For to his humble Handmaids ſtate
He ſhow'd regard, when 't was depreſt,
All Ages ſhall from henceforth judge
Me Happy, and ſhall call me Bleſt.

He that is Great hath done to me
Great things, and Holy is his Name;
His Mercy through all Ages is,
To them that fear him, ſtill the ſame,

He with his Arm his ſtrength hath ſhow'd,
Confounded what the proud men thought;
Put down the Mighty from their Seat,
And rais'd them who were ſet at nought.

He fill'd the Hungry Souls with good,
The Full and Rich for want complain'd;
His Mercy he has call'd to mind,
And Iſrael his help has gain'd.

L 5 The

The Promise to our Fathers made
So long before, in which God stood
Engag'd to Abraham and his Seed,
Is all performed and made good.

Hymn III.

Nunc Dimittis.

(*The Song of* Simeon. *Luc.* 2. 29.)

I Now can leave this World, and die
In Peace and quiet rest;
Since that mine Eyes, O Lord, have been
With thy Salvation blest.
The Prophecies are all fulfill'd,
Thy Promises are true;
And thy Mysterious Love disclos'd
In all the Peoples view.

All the dark shadows fly away,
Now this bright Sun appears;
Whose saving Light the Gentile World
With unknown comfort cheers.
Well may the long expected sight
Make Isr'els Joys abound;
Before with special Favours grac'd,
But now with Glory Crown'd.

Hymn

Hymn IV.

(Out of several Passages of the Revelations.)

ALl ye that serve the Lord, his Name R.15.5.
   See that ye celebrate;
And ye that fear him, sing aloud
   His praise, both small and great.
O thou great Ruler of the World, R.19.3.
   Thy works our wonder raise.
Thou Blessed King of Saints, how True
   And Righteous are thy ways!

Who would not fear and praise thy Name
   Thou onely Holy one?
The World will worship thee, to whom
   Thy Judgments are made known.
Most Holy, Holy, Holy, Lord Ca. 4. 8.
   Almighty is thy Name;
Which was before all time, and is,
   And shall be still the same.

Al Glory, Pow'r and Honour, thou Ve. 11.
   Art worthy to receive;
For all things by thy Pow'r were made,
   And by thy Pleasure live.
To thee of right, O Lamb of God, C. 5.12.
   Riches and Pow'r belong;
Wisedom and Honour, Glory, Strength,
   And every praising Song.

                                 Thou

Ve. 9.   Thou, as our Sacrifice, waſt ſlain,
         And by thy pretious Blood,
       From every Tongue and Nation, haſt
       Redeem'd us unto God.
V. 13.   Bleſſing and Honour, Glory, Pow'r,
        By all in Earth and Heav'n,
      To him that ſits upon the Throne,
      And to the Lamb, be giv'n.

Hymn V.

Te Deum.

(*As the* 100 *Pſalm.*)

O God we praiſe thee, and we own
    Thee to be Lord and King alone.
All the whole Earth doth worſhip thee,
Thou Father from Eternity.

To thee all Angels loudly cry,
The Heav'ns and all the Pow'rs on high;
Cherubs and Seraphins proclaim,
And cry thrice Holy to thy Name.

Lord God of Hoſts, thy Preſence bright,
Fills Heav'n and Earth with beauteous Light.
Th' Apoſtles glorious Company,
The Prophets Fellowſhip, praiſe thee.

                            The

The Crowned Martyrs Noble Host,
The Holy Church in every Coast,
Thine Infinite perfections own,
Father of Majesty unknown.

Giving all Adoration
Unto thy true and onely Son:
And to the Holy Ghost, from whom
As the sole Spring, our Comforts come.

O Christ, thou Glorious King, we own
Thee to be God's Eternal Son:
Who, our deliv'rance to obtain,
Didst not the Virgins Womb disdain.

When Deaths sharp sting destroy'd by thee
Gave thee a Glorious Victory,
Heav'ns Gate, that Entrance had deny'd,
Then to believers opened wide.

Part. II.

At God's Right hand thou, Lord, art plac'd,
And with thy Father's Glory grac'd;
And we believe the Day will come,
When thou as Judge shalt pass our doom.

Promote, we pray, thy Servants Good
Redeemed with thy pretious Blood:
Among thy Saints make them ascend
To Glory that shall never end.

Thy

Thy people with Salvation Crown;
Bleſs thoſe, O God, that are thine own;
Govern and lift them up on high.
Thee, Lord, we daily magnify.

Thy Name we worſhip and adore,
Ever, When Time ſhall be no more;
Vouchſafe this Day to keep us pure,
From harms and wilfull ſins ſecure,

O let thy mercy, Lord, deſcend
On us, whoſe hopes on thee depend:
Lord, ſince my Truſt is fix'd on thee,
O let me ne'er confounded be.

Gloria Patri.

(*To the Common Tunes.*)

TO thee, O Father, to the Son
    And Holy Ghoſt, we give
Glory that was of old, is now,
And ſhall this World ſurvive,

Glo-

Gloria Patri.

(As the 100 Psalm.)

TO thee, O Father, to the Son
    And Holy Ghost, whom we adore,
Be Glory, as it was of old ,
Is now, and shall be Evermore.

An

Words less Common,	Their Signification.
Celebrate	make renowned.
Detracting	lessening due praise.
Diffusive	spreading wide.
Fluid	yielding.
Impetuous	violent.
Lovver Sphere	meaner condition.
Orbs, Spheres	bodies of a round form
Perturbation	disturbance, trouble.
Precipice	dovvnfall.
Recesses	retirements, places out of vievv.
Revere	to reverence, stand in avve.
Rude mass	unshapen matter.
Theam	subject of discourse.
Uncessant	never ceasing.
Unexhausted	never dravvn dry

AN

ALPHABETICAL TABLE,
whereby any Pſalm is found,
knovving its beginning.

B.

C.

E.

M   Give

Re-

To

THE END.